Pea Patches
and
Butterbean Fields

VICKI BAYLIS

ISBN 978-1-64114-907-5 (paperback)
ISBN 978-1-64114-908-2 (digital)

Christian Faith Publishing, Inc.
832 Park Avenue
Meadville, PA 16335
www.christianfaithpublishing.com

Printed in the United States of America

It is with much love that I dedicate this one to my mother, Missie Yevonne Perkins. Unknowingly, she taught her children how to be tough when the world around them gets rocky. The South is not all about sipping sweet tea in the shade. Sometimes, you must bear the heat from the pea patches and butterbean fields. It is a good mother that teaches her children how to do both.

Contents

1

Dogsledding in Mississippi

I'll start this story by telling you that my daddy was a Navy man. That being said, it meant that brother Bill knew the meaning of doing chores. One of those chores was keeping the yard in tip-top shape. In fact, before they actually unhooked our brand new four-teen-by-seventy-foot mobile home at the trailer park in Oak Grove, my daddy had Bill pushing the lawn mower. Our new trailer park lot had been vacant for quite some time, and the yard was in need of a mowing. After the professionals unhooked our dark-green-and-walnut-colored metal mansion, our daddy then noticed all the over-grown grass underneath it. "Bill, Vicki, y'all get some scissors and trim that mess," he said. Keep in mind, this event took place before Weed eaters were invented. Let me tell you a pair of scissors will give a whole new meaning to the words *fourteen-by-seventy foot*. It took us a week to get the grass cut under there. I believe the medical term nowadays is called child abuse, but we just called it chores. Of course, you know what all those chores did to us? It made us productive adults who, in turn, taught our own kids the meaning of chores.

Halfway through our character-building adventure, my daddy borrowed an electric handheld grass trimmer from one of his bud-dies. Kind of looked like a cake batter mixer you would find in a kitchen, only at the end of it was a clipper blade. Although it prob-ably trimmed about three inches at a time, it was way faster than a pair of scissors. Sad to say, Bill and I fought over whose turn it was with the high-tech wonder. A few days after we got the underside of the trailer manicured to Dad's expectations, he had to take a gun to a big rattlesnake living under there. Please stop and ask me where my little sister was while Bill and I were belly crawling around on our stomachs with a pair of scissors. Princess Terri was inside eating snacks and watching TV. I'm sure my memory is correct when I say every once in a while, she would stick her head out the door and say something like, "They not cutting, Momma."

My father's being a union electrician by trade only made matters worse. Needless to say, my daddy's tool shed was organized. O-R-G-A-N-I-Z-E-D! "Don't mess with my tools." There was no getting away with losing one of his screwdrivers either 'cause everything was hung on a pegboard, outlined with a black magic marker. Not kidding. When any of his tools were missing, it looked like a crime scene was being investigated.

I remember, one day, Daddy came home with a new rope. "Don't mess with my rope, you hear?" And we did hear the warning all right. At least up until the day we got off the school bus and my brother Bill saw a horse tied up at the end of our street. A horse in the trailer park was just too good to pass up. Now we don't remember why someone had a horse tied up, but there it was—all alone—and calling my brother's name. Next thing Bill knew, he and his buddies were hauling that horse over to a set of abandon concrete steps. Turns out that horse did not allow free rides.

Dad's new rope enters the story here. It wasn't long before the horse-riding adventure turned into a dogsledding event that will no doubt go down in history. I'd like to enter into evidence the very reason all this happened. Bill had a friend named Roy, and Roy's grandparents lived up north where it snows all the time. Everybody with me so far? One Christmas, Roy got a sled from those Northerners, which as a grownup may sound like an odd gift for a young'un living in Mississippi and in a trailer park, no doubt. But to a boy, it was a cool gift. All he needed to do was wait for the snow, right? Or maybe not.

This is where the story begins to end badly for the new rope. Believe it or not, the horse turned down their sled-riding idea. While the boys were sitting on the sled, the horse would not budge at all, but as soon as they climbed off, that horse would take off, pulling the sled without a problem. Let the record reflect the fast-trotting horse left the trailer park, weaving in and out of busy traffic on Oak Grove Road, dragging Roy's Christmas present and Dad's new rope behind him.

If this adventure had only ended here, then Dad would have never known his new rope had been missing from his tool shed for a few hours that day. But it didn't. For Roy had a big dog. "Let's make a dogsledding team," someone suggested. And they did. Bill and his buddies rounded up every stray dog they could find hanging around the trailer park. Luck was on their side for there was a female dog that already had a big crew following her around—perfect. To those young boys, it appeared she was a natural-born leader. Let me stop here and ask if I actually have to tell you why all those boy dogs were following her? Everybody still with me so far?

It took a minute or two to get their sledding team tied up and ready for this adventure of a lifetime. You know what happened next? Everybody on their dogsledding team started fighting. And since everybody was tied together, it was the dogfight of the century. Turns out not only did those stray dogs not want to pull a sled, but they all of a sudden didn't want to be friends anymore either. "We got to help the dogs," someone yelled. It was at this moment Bill realized that Dad's new rope was not faring too well. "Dogs nothing, what about the rope?" my brother was panicking.

There was nothing left to do but risk life and limb. One dog at a time, Bill made a mad dash into the tangled up mess cutting them loose. Let's just say when it was all over, my dad had many ropes—all different kind of sizes too. It was the last time Bill wanted anything to do with a sled. Besides, now none of them had a rope. Dogsledding in Mississippi is just not a thing, or least not in our trailer park. If you don't believe me, just ask my brother Bill.

2

I Shall Make the Dressing

There comes a time in every woman's life when she finally decides to put the big girl panties on and cook the Thanksgiving meal herself. This was my year—age fifty. Up until this blessed event, I relied on my mother and my mother-in-law to do the honors. Of course, I would always be assigned a vegetable or two; some years, I even advanced up to dessert. I am not ashamed to admit, but on the years I was in charge of paper products were heaven-on-earth years. Hey, don't judge.

Our family made the decision to volunteer at a local shelter on the big day. Like with almost everything I do, I tend to speak first and consult the brain later. "I'll make the dressing." In horror, I realized the sentence had jumped out of my mouth—wait, what? Honestly, I have no idea where those words came from for I have never made dressing in my life. But I said it out loud, and the lady in charge wrote it down, and it soon became law. Oh sure, I could have called her back and declared my stupidity, but actually, admitting I am not really a true Southern woman is a fate far worse. I mean, after all, what Southern woman cannot make dressing?

I put a call in to my mother. "It's time, Mother. It's time." The countdown had begun, and every day, I would wake up and note, "Oh, what have I done? What have I done?" I can't make dressing. I can't. I am going to be the volunteer that ends up poisoning everyone with her dressing. Oh, the horror it will be! I can hear it now: "This dressing is terrible."

A couple of days before the blessed event, believe it or not, I made matters worse. "Hey, since I am making dressing anyway, I'll just cook Thanksgiving for us too." Seven or so trips to Walmart, I was finally prepared. Let the cooking begin.

And it did. All sixty-two-hundred hours of it, not really that long, but it felt like it by the time I finished. Y'all think back to your childhood days when the cartoon character was flinging things up into the air: once he stopped the chaos his project was complete—well, that is what it looked like in my kitchen. Timers were going off everywhere. Eggshells were lying all over the counter tops. Based on the evidence left behind in my kitchen, I was in the midst of the sweet potato massacre of 2014, not to mention the onions. Every time I turned around, I was crying, mostly due to the onions but sometimes due to being overwhelmed by the cooking. I seriously thought about having a meltdown a couple of times. If it had not been for the main man, I would have.

"Mother, where are you?" I called her in a panic.

"I'm pulling into the subdivision, why?" she asked.

"Well, bring your car down into my driveway."

Why, yes, that was me carrying a pan of dressing outside, standing in the yard, waiting on my mother to pass by. I am not ashamed.

"Taste this. What's missing?" I handed her a spoonful of cornbread dressing.

"Add some more sage," she said, and then she wheeled her car back out of my drive.

That brings me to this point in my story—what in the world is sage? And when my mother's recipe calls for a "little bit of sage," what in the world is a "little bit?" I never ever want to hear those words again. With the last sprinkle of sage, we commenced to cleaning up the kitchen. Unless you have experienced cooking the Thanksgiving meal, you will not understand the true meaning of "used every pan in the house."

Somewhere between the mixing up stage and the actual cooking stage, I lay down in the bed and cried. My whole body ached. I was tired and whiny. If I could get my hands on a few pilgrims and Indians, we'd have a little talk. As far as I was concerned, the government could wipe this holiday off the calendar for good. I never wanted to see it again.

You want to know what happened next? We gathered around the table, and the main man said the blessing. We passed the butter and the cranberry sauce. We piled all those vegetables and casseroles on our plates. "Mom, this dressing is just like Granny Perkins's dressing," my children said. I watched as my family laughed. We reminisced about the past, and we planned for the future. We drank coffee. We ate pecan pie. We played cards. We took pictures.

It was then that I realized something. Thanksgiving is not necessarily about the turkey and vegetables or even the desserts. It's about the togetherness that follows all those dirty dishes. Next up is the beloved Christmas dinner. I've never been completely in charge of cooking Christmas dinner. You know what? I won't be either.

3

Rebekah's Confession

You all know by now my daughter is a teacher. She is an excellent teacher too if I do say so myself. When she moved off to the coast to teach the young'uns down there, I would go and spend a day or two with her once a week. Always the first thing on the list to do after school let out was to find a restaurant. On this particular day, it was the Hibachi Grill. Next, we always head to Walmart. She thinks I am just buying her groceries to be nice. Truth be told, it is because she is a vegetarian, so when I visit her house, I end up having to eat twigs and berries. Her cabinet rarely has real food—you know, cookies and brownies and such. Always a fun time pushing the buggy through the grocery store, talking and laughing and shopping.

Somewhere between the restaurant and the groceries, she and I were talking about a child who was sassing her that day—not one of her students, mind you. She knows how to handle that situation. This incident caused her to recall a "sin" from her years' past—age eight to be exact. I was horrified to learn the crime in question took place at Vacation Bible School. She can still remember vividly the Bible school theme and everything.

Before I go any further, raise your hand if you have ever told your children, "You better be on your best behavior." or the ever popular one when I was growing up, "Don't you dare embarrass the family name." So at the age of twenty-five, my daughter says, "Mom, I got in trouble at VBS. My teacher was passing out papers, and she thought I snatched it from her hand. I didn't, Mom."

Now her teacher was none other than Mrs. Leigh-Anne Strahan, the pastor's wife. "Rebekah, I know your mother taught you better than that," said the wife of my preacher. My preacher! Apparently, the look she received from her VBS teacher and the shame of getting in trouble still haunts my child to this day. As any good Southern mother would do, I gasped. Oh, the shame. Even though it was more than a decade later, I felt a rebaptism was in order. I am thankful I did not know this information until now.

I don't know why, but my daughter decided to confess all her sins right there in Walmart. Three times—three times—she has gotten into trouble three other times in her childhood by someone who was not her relative: her kindergarten teacher, her eighth grade teacher, and her ninth grade teacher. Who is this child?

In Rebekah's defense, she still to this day denies shooting Officer John's daughter with a water gun on beach day in kindergarten. Although I did not witness the crime, I was there and did in fact take a picture of my little criminal enduring time-out on the sidewalk.

Thankfully, the ninth grade incident was expunged from her record even though she suffered irreversible damage. The crime was arguing with a teacher. Who knew having to sit in time-out in the hallway as a fifteen-year-old is harder to recover from than when you are five? "Teacher was wrong. I was right." If memory serves her correctly, she declares the teacher got in trouble too. Probably not. I have no knowledge of the incident in question. I tend to side with the teachers anyway. It's probably the reason I didn't hear about it in the first place.

In regard to the eighth grade incident, she has decided to plead the fifth. The fact that we go to church with the teacher and are Facebook friends, she has decided to not reveal the details. "Just know there was an incident," she confessed and then rolled her buggy away. I don't need to know the details anyhow. I'll be too busy avoiding eye contact with said teacher from here on out.

Back to the Vacation Bible School incident, I think she learned her lesson. For years, she thought sinning at church meant automatically being sent to Hades, bypassing a talk with the Lord altogether. I guess that is worse than any time-out. Loving my strong-willed daughter—criminal past and all.

4

The Christmas Tree of Memories

When the children were toddlers, decorating the Christmas tree was a bit tricky at our house. For years, only the top half of my tree was decorated with the pretty ornaments—the store-bought ones. After all, they were much too valuable to break. Scattered all over the lower half of the tree were the ones the children would give me. Every year, they would add at least two handmade ornaments to our collections—one from the school and then another from their Sunday school class.

It's been years since I opened the plastic storage container full of the handmade treasures. This year, I decided to bring them out and use them for old time's sake. Each silver hook held a precious memory, and as I reached into the plastic box, I would smile and tear up a little.

There are little thumbprints scattered around my tree and pictures of my children encircled with glitter. Little beads held together by fishing string, a colorful construction paper chain that has long since faded, a Styrofoam peanut chain too. A little bell made from an egg carton and covered with tinfoil has taken its place on a branch once again. There are some Disney characters. And sprinkled all over this year's tree are little ornaments that my mother-in-law took the time to make with all her grandkids. I see Barney, the purple creature, from many moons ago. I'm happy to say that song—y'all remember the song, right. Well, it finally escapes my memory. I see many Popsicle sticks painted up to look like reindeer and Santa Clauses.

15

Many of the ornaments have the years dated on the backs. Those not dated make me wish a thousand times over that I had taken the few extra seconds to grab a pen. To all you young parents—date everything. Trust me when I say you will forget many of the precious details.

I realized now the ornaments on the bottom half of the tree were far more valuable than what was on the top half. I wish someone had told me that years ago. So I want to tell all you young parents out there to put the handmade ornaments on the top half. You can always buy the store-bought ones, but the little hands that make the most beautiful of all treasures do not stay little long. Cherish the little hands and the memories they make. Merry Christmas—2014.

5

Covington County

Every once in a while, a brilliant idea will pop into my head. In this case, it was an idea about a book—I would travel to each of the eighty-two counties in Mississippi and write about the details. Cousin Cindy and I placed all the county names in a jar. When time came to plan a trip, we would draw one out. This made it fun not knowing where we would end up on the weekend trip. I realize now with a budget like mine—a nonexistent one—this type of book would take twenty years to complete, so I will just add the story here.

As luck would have it, Covington County was the first name out of the jar. It's just one county over, and we have been there time and time again. What could we possibly find new to do there? I asked around, and the general consensus was we must canoe down the Okatoma River. Oh sure, that would have been awesome except it was winter and twelve degrees outside. I'm afraid there is not enough manpower in this county to get me in a little boat in cold water. Of course, we could have toured Mitchell Farms among the pumpkins if it had been October, but it was January, and it was cold outside.

I guess you can say we ended up eating our way through this county. Yep, there is some fine eating in these parts. We found ourselves in the middle of nowhere and sitting at a table at the Salem Opera House. Years ago, it was part of a schoolhouse auditorium. If you look closely enough, you will notice the floor slants just a little. We had the sweetest waitress, and she informed us of the Covington

County Chamber of Commerce brochure that was sitting on the counter next to the cash register. Perfect!

Fine eating, I tell you, fine eating. Each one of us had something different. I, of course, had catfish. Anytime Cindy can order crab cakes, she does. That man she married couldn't decide, so he ordered the seafood platter—a little bit of everything. My main man was complaining about his knees hurting right before he ordered, so Cindy and I diagnosed him with gout and told him to order a salad. He refused and ordered the steak instead. We put our medical degrees back inside our purses and reached for the basket of hush puppies that had arrived to the table. Yum. Meal number one had commenced, and afterward, we slowly crawled back to our cabin.

We found the most beautiful place overlooking the Okatoma River, like living with Laura Ingalls in *Little House on the Prairie*. It was complete with loft. There were no TV, no washing machine, and no dishwasher. There was nothing but peace and quiet. You can certainly say it was authentic all right. Let's just say a candle would have had trouble staying lit in this place. Between the draft and the hot flashes my cousin was having, we gave that thermostat a good workout.

If you are looking for a perfect getaway from today's hustle and bustle, this is the place. It was so peaceful. You could actually hear the rippling of the water as it flowed around the bend. I could have sat on the back porch, rocking in those chairs for hours on end, if it hadn't been twelve degrees outside. But the cold weather didn't dampen our spirits any. Cindy and I have been playing cards since our college days, and we decided to spend the time doing just that.

If I can be honest with you, I need to point out a major flaw in this great county. Whoever set up the GPS must have been drinking a little because it ain't right. Case in point when we set out to meet a local potter. When the GPS said, "You have arrived at your destination," and your car is sitting in the middle of a cow pasture, something is wrong. "Do y'all see anything but cows?"

Claudia KA Cartee has lived in Seminary since the early seventies. I hope we were not the only ones to get lost trying to find her gallery. As we eased our vehicle down the little winding road leading up to her place, Cindy and I checked to make sure we had cell phone service. I can't tell you how many times my cousin and I have driven ourselves into a *Silence of the Lambs* sequel by mistake.

Let me just say, Mrs. Cartee's place was awesome. It was beautiful, peaceful, almost heavenly. She welcomed us as if we were long-lost cousins stopping by for coffee. The knowledge this artist shared with us was priceless. How on earth did we not know anything about her? It was right here in Seminary, Mississippi, of all places. If I were rich, she would still be bagging up pieces of pottery for me to take home. But I'm not rich. I spent almost an hour picking out two pieces of pottery. Let me tell you that was a hard decision because everything was beautiful. Do you want to know what happened next? She let us see inside her studio. Awesome.

We visited with her until almost lunchtime. In this county, lunch means one thing and one thing only to me—Main Street Café in Collins. I blame their home-cooking buffet solely for my pants not fitting this morning. There is something about their fried chicken that will make you lose all your Southern manners. I don't care who sees me going back for seconds. Lord, have mercy, the rice and gravy, I just want to stand at the buffet table with a big spoon. After all these years of going there, I do not know how I missed the loaded baked potato salad. I had to have a little talk with Jesus when I found myself wanting to lick the plate. Don't get me started on the desserts. We all needed a nap after that. We actually moaned while putting our seat belts back on.

Next stop on our tour through Covington County was Hot Coffee, Mississippi. Actually, it was more like a slow drive-by with a wave of our hand than an actual stop. We did, however, stop the car at McDonald's Store—a country mini-mall that's been around since the thirties located right down the road. They had a little bit of everything: milk, bread, tools, hats, and boots. We found the lady behind the cash register very friendly. It seems everyone in this county makes you feel welcomed. I don't know about you guys, but I kind of like that. Makes you want to come back.

It was somewhere around here we got lost on the back roads—completely lost. All the GPS would say was you can't get there from here. Well, it didn't use those exact words, but that's what "no results found" meant to me. We were never so happy as when we stumbled into the big city of Mt. Olive—all three minutes of it. Sadly, before this day was over, we would be lost in the deep woods of this county once again.

Somehow, we managed to drive right into the world of Mr. Diehl at Roger's Basketry. Man, oh, man, what a character he is. I could sit and talk with him for hours. In fact, my main man and that man my cousin married did just that. They talked about farming, and tractors, and buggies, and all things manly. It was the nicest visit.

While the menfolk talked and talked, Cindy and I were bursting at the seams to get inside his basket store. I'll have you know, we touched every one of those handmade baskets trying to pick just the right one. I got mine sitting on a table in the kitchen. At first, I was going to put it next to my husband's recliner, but he would just get it dirty, and then I'd have to hide his body somewhere for messing up my beautiful basket.

Speaking of kitchens, years ago, Mr. Diehl and his wife owned a restaurant right there at his home place. I wish I had known about it. I definitely would have pulled a chair up to a table there. He was kind enough to show us the restaurant too, even lighting one of the gas chandeliers. Yes, sir, you read that correctly. In keeping with his faith, there is no electricity at his place. I find that fascinating. I guess my favorite thing I took away from my visit with him was some of his family's recipes. Inside one of the cookbooks is a poem about thanking God for dirty dishes. I won't share the poem here because I don't know who to give credit for the words. I can't wait to serve some of the recipes with family at my kitchen table.

I will say finding Graham's Fish Camp was like finding a needle in a haystack. Eventually, we did. Let me tell you, by the time we wobbled out of there, we all had unbuttoned our pants. There was one thing we learned after that meal, and it was we needed to get the heck out of this county while our clothes still fit. Before bedtime, Cindy and I were wearing sweatpants and sipping Nyquil. Why, you ask? Because on Highway 49, right before you get to the community of Lux, there is a fruit stand that sells Randazzo's King Cakes from

New Orleans. Do not stop and buy one of them. They are like crack. We bought two and a bag of boiled peanuts. Lord, have mercy, this county is killing us one spoonful at a time.

Now let me get to the Nyquil. As we were all gathered around the card table, a creature of some sort began scattering around on the porch. From the sound of it, it was as big as a dog with claws a mile long. We dared not mention it to the men for they would have surely opened the doors to investigate it. It was best to let the creature alone. I'm sure Pa Ingalls would have shot it for supper. But this is where I draw the line with our rustic, down-to-earth, country-living-in-the-woods adventure. Unless that creature was advanced enough to open the cabin doors, I didn't want to know anything else. The Nyquil would help us forget all about it within forty-five minutes or so. And it did.

Somewhere in Seminary was a sign that read "Saturday Night Chitlin," and our hopes of trying one of them was cut short because Cindy was needed back at home. One of their cows was having a little trouble dropping a calf. Thank goodness! Honestly, I was getting a little worried about that chitlin anyway.

Covington County was a blast—good food, good people, pretty county. Just remember to bring a map and maybe a compass.

6

I May Have to Leave Town

I may have to leave town. I will miss y'all. You may recall my fear of MRI machines, bad weather, and needles, but today, I have sunk to a new low. Oh, the shame. Y'all ever heard the saying, "Don't embarrass the family name." Well, today, I did just that. This whole fiasco started when I fell into that hole in the parking lot of a fast-food restaurant. It was bad enough that I looked as though I was three sheets to the wind doing so, but today, I made that incident look like I was a member of Disney on Ice—gracefully gliding across the parking lot.

Let me begin with my trip to the MRI machine this past Saturday. Since there was a little incident the last time I crawled into the tube, the medical professionals suggested I be medicated this time. I agreed. I got two Xanax pills. First, let me say that I have never taken one before, so they gave me one to take the day before my test—a practice run, so to speak. Well, let me tell you about Xanax. Xanax equals coma. I lost two whole days of my life—gone just like that. How anyone functions on that stuff is beyond me. But the good news is I didn't worry about the tornadoes going through the area while I was in that tube. Even when the x-ray technician said, "Stop moving around in there," I was like, *What? Dude, I'm in a coma over here. I can't be moving.*

Now let me get to the part where I embarrassed the family name. I'm sitting in the office, and in walks my doctor. Surely, he is about to tell me I will need some kind of drastic knee surgery to cure this leg I have been dragging around for the last two months. He pulls up the MRI results so I can look at them too as he explains things. I am just nodding along as he is telling me this and that. Being untrained in the reading of MRIs, I am looking at the inside of my leg and think-ing, *Lord, have mercy, that thing looks horrific. It must be bad.*

But you know what? He said it was nothing but arthritis and a little tear in my meniscus, a very little tear that didn't warrant surgery at this time either. You know what else that man said? He had a cure. Yep, he did. He could fix me up right there in his office. All I needed was a shot. *A shot in my knee?* Well, it is obvious he and I are not on the same page at all. I ain't getting no shot and especially not one in my knee. *Well, will you looky there. It's a miracle. I am healed.* We can wrap this visit up. Tell that nurse to give me my paperwork. I'll be on my way.

But in all seriousness, I am tired of hurting. So I agreed to the procedure. He walks out to tell the nurse. That gave me just enough time to change my mind—five times. I stick my head out of the room to tell them that somebody needs to call my anesthesiologist because we are going to need a little anesthesia up in this room.

It is here that I began to lose all dignity. Apparently, I reached the point where I no longer could use proper medical terminology, and I looked them folks in the eyes and said, "I'm gonna need to tinkle before we get started with that needle." Oh, the shame. Yep, I just told my orthopedic surgeon, a medical professional of no less than ten years of medical training, that I had to tinkle. So I did what any good Southern woman would have done at that point in time. I walked out of that room—down the hall and out the door. As my doctor politely opened the door for me to escape, he more than likely thought I was not coming back. I then proceeded to walk across the waiting room, grabbed my husband's hand, and reminded him about the "for better or worse" papers he signed twenty-seven years ago. He is not missing out on this little party, for sure.

We are all sitting around my knee and by we, I mean me, my husband, the nurse, the doctor, and Jesus because I have called him down to this here room too. It is here that it happened. I saw the nee-dle. Hold it! Wait! I changed my mind. There ain't no way that needle is going into my body. Nope. Jesus can go on back to heaven—sorry, I wasted His time, but this ain't happening.

But it did. I am here to testify to the fine medical skills of my doctor. He did good. The only thing that did not survive was my pride and my nursing professionalism. All I can say now is thank the good Lord we have HIPAA.

7

Thank Goodness for Mimis

Did you know *mimi* is another word for a grandmother? Today, I met one of the greatest mimis of all time, according to a little boy at the Lucedale stockyard. I'll get back to mimi in a minute, but first, let me recall a conversation I had with Cousin Cindy yesterday.

"I'm going to sell rabbits, pheasants, and turkeys at the stock-yard, wanna go?" said Cindy.

"Shoot yeah!"

I mean, how can I turn that down? I have never done that before, and besides, it sounds like a barrel of fun.

"I need to get there at eight," Cindy continued.

"All right, count me in. Can't wait."

"You do know that means we leave the house at six-forty-five in the morning?" my husband added to the conversation.

"Wait, what?"

You may recall my inability to be a ray of sunshine so early in the day. The way I look at it is, ever since the Heavenly Father put the big ball of fire in the sky, he had not once needed my help getting it up there. Let me have my two cups of coffee in bed and then all will be right in my little world. This morning, as Cindy and I are standing around the stockyard parking lot watching God put the sun in the right place, it began to rain. Yep, rain. I'm here to tell you rabbit selling is not as fun as you might think when you are wearing two jackets, gloves, and toting a big umbrella. But as any red-blooded Mississippi farmer will tell you, the farmwork must go on. Besides, the stockyard was fixing to start the bidding on the sheep, goats, and pigs, and I was not missing any of that fun. Let the rabbit selling begin.

One by one, people started mingling past our table. Although most of the menfolk stepped up their pace quite a bit once, they realized our kennels were full of pet rabbits. And by pets, we were quick to point out these babies were not for your kitchen pots and pans.

We were cold and waited patiently for just the right buyers. Then it happened. A little boy took a peek inside our kennels. He was the most precious little boy, complete with jeans and boots—a miniature cowboy in the making, no doubt. We asked him if he wanted to take home a few rabbits—he did. While we were waiting for the family to catch up with this fast-paced cowboy, we jokingly said, "If you got a hundred dollar bill, you can buy all these rabbits."

You want to know what that little cowboy said? "I don't, but my mimi does. Hold on."

Only Mimi didn't really want to buy rabbits. "You don't need those rabbits." She was quick to point out to our new rabbit buyer.

"Oh yes, I do, Mimi," the sweet-talking cowboy began to plead his rabbit case.

The little shopper got busy walking up and down the table of rabbits, taking his time in picking out the most perfect additions to Mimi's family, for not just any rabbit would do, you know. Let me tell you, it wasn't long before Mimi was finding a box—a box big enough for two of those little darlings. Everyone was pleased with this rabbit-buying adventure, well, everyone except maybe Mimi. After those fluffy things were loaded up in the back of Mimi's big truck, the little cowboy walked back over to my husband and stuck his hand out. "Thank you, sir," he said as he shook hands like a grown man. It appeared to everyone around our table that this cowboy was being raised right and this mimi was doing an awesome job at being a mimi. Thank heaven for mimis.

8

Happy Valentine's Day

In keeping with our mission to visit every county in the state, the next two drawn from the jar were Marshall and Benton. Valentine weekend seemed to be the perfect timing for such an adventure. "Welcome to Holly Springs. Y'all hurry up and look because we close this town down at 4:00 p.m. sharp." Well, dang. I wish I had known this tidbit of information earlier because we had just spent the morning slowly moseying up the highways from Hattiesburg. I will admit I was a little sad we didn't get to look and touch everything in the Marshall County Historical Museum in Holly Springs. The building is full of history, and I wanted to read about it all. On the third floor was a room dedicated to yellow fever. Scary. I kept my hands down and held my breath in there. I certainly didn't want to awake that sleeping dog.

Also on the third floor was giant dollhouses made for children. It made me think about the little girls that played with them years ago. I actually found myself wanting to rearrange all the tiny pieces of furniture. I laughed a little when I compared these fine pieces of woodwork to what Santa Claus brought my daughter when she was into all things Barbie.

My husband will be the first to tell you he is not a carpenter, so when our daughter wanted a house for her dolls, he set out to build one. And build one, he did. The store-bought ones were not in our budget that Christmas. Since Santa was to bring this mansion, we secretly constructed it out of view. Let me tell you, he went to hammering, and I went to painting. With the help of some leftover carpet and flooring scrapes, this jewel was right up there with the looks of Graceland or the White House—if only they were crack houses. When the time came to move Barbie's new shindig to the room with the Christmas tree, it would not budge—it weighed a ton—once again proving we are not carpenters. I will say Barbie did not have to worry about tornadoes or hurricanes, though.

Anyway, back to my story. The Audubon Society has three thousand beautiful landscaped acres and the Antebellum Davis Home. At least the lady at the Chamber of Commerce testified to that fact. We, on the other hand, cannot give testimony because it closed down at 4:00 p.m. with the rest of the town.

Making matters even worse was the fact it was a holiday weekend. Of course, we arrived too late to enjoy the professional tours offered. Being from the South, we can make do with any situation, though. We grabbed a map to all the antebellum homes—shoot, we will make the tour ourselves. How hard can that be, right? This proved to be mistake number two. That man my cousin married was the tour bus driver, and my husband was our tour guide.

Cousin Cindy and I needed Dramamine when our tour bus finally stopped. I would like to apologize for all the illegal U-turns and backed-up traffic jams our vehicle may have caused. I'm glad I didn't pay good money for that chauffeured experience—it was absolutely worthless. I'm still having flashbacks—stop, watch out for that truck, turn here, wait, that's a one-way street, back up, hurry, we gonna get run over, I don't think that was legal. Oh, the horror Cindy and I endued from the back seat.

Which leads me to tell you what happened later on that night. We found a little restaurant open in the town's square. This place was full of character. I'm sad to say it is here I decided to embarrass the family name. Everyone who knows me knew it would happen sooner or later, and Marshall County, Mississippi, just so happened to be the lucky place. You see, this restaurant had a karaoke stage. That's right—karaoke. And keeping with my "try everything once" philosophy, I decided to march myself on up to that stage. I mean, seriously, if the little kids could do it, certainly, I could too. Besides, no one knew me in this neck of the woods.

If there were ever any doubts to my singing ability, I cleared it up that evening. I can't sing! Didn't matter in this little town, though. Those townsfolk made me feel as if I was just as talented as the original Patsy Cline. To the horror of the main man, Cousin Cindy, and that man she married, the DJ asked me to sing another one—and I did! I'm sure when he asked for an encore, he had no idea it would actually be worse than the first performance, but it was. I can now check karaoke off my list of things to do. Loved it. My apologies to Patsy.

We giggled as we walked back to our bed-and-breakfast. Speaking of our lodging, it was absolutely the best stay. It was like a home away from home. Our hostess was Lisa, and like so many of us self-employed folks, she too was chief, cook, and bottle washer. Our conversation was more like catching up with the relatives.

As Lisa was giving a tour of the bed-and-breakfast, she happened to mention that my bedroom's furniture was built in 1840. Talk about ruining a romantic Valentine's weekend—be still, don't move, don't even snore. Our family will not be the ones who break the antique bed. As bedtime approached, the bed was not my only fear—I begin to worry about seeing ghost. What if they didn't want us sleeping in their bed?

If I had any of my dignity left, I lost it when we walked back across the street to have breakfast the next morning. Lucky for us, a new crew was serving the tables, and no one seemed to recall my short-lived singing career.

Now let me tell you about Benton County. I must confess for a couple of months, Cousin Cindy and I searched the World Wide Web looking for hotels, events, and interesting things to do in this county—could not find a thing. Even talked to some folks from up that way—still nothing. So we just jumped in the car with a map and headed out to explore.

A quick trip through Ashland, Hickory Flat, and then Potts Camp revealed what looked like nothing but quiet peaceful towns. Of course, it was a Saturday, and we probably could have just missed all their hustle and bustle of the weekdays. It was a place where everybody probably knows everybody. That can be a good thing—and perhaps a bad thing too, certainly, if you are trying to hide poor judgment calls such as really bad karaoke singing.

There are a couple of lakes for fishing and camping. Our next trip up, we will certainly bring the fishing poles and stay in one of the cabins we found. Along the slowly driven roads, we made several U-turns when things caught our eyes—a log cabin, a beautiful pasture, an old barn, and a historic marker revealing something from the past. We even stumbled upon a field with an outdoor museum full of brightly colored tractors—right there in the middle of nowhere. There were fourteen perfectly restored old-timey tractors. The menfolk took their time looking at all the features and talking about how things have changed since then. I don't know the first thing about tractors, but they sure were pretty to look at. It led me to another one of life's goals—I need to drive one.

In Potts Camp, we found a little country store called This and That. It is where we met Ken, the owner. We all gathered around a wood stove and talked like we had known each other for years and were just catching up on things. Benton County was quiet, peaceful, hilly, and beautiful.

We enjoyed our journey through these two counties. It's a good place to practice your singing—talent is not necessary. Happy Valentine's Day 2015.

9

Well, There He Goes

It's always an adventure when we help out at my cousin's farm. Yesterday, they were hosting a petting zoo party for a three-year-old little boy and his group of friends. Of course, we wanted to help. As tradition dictates, we strike up conversations with each one of our guests. It's a Southern thing, I reckon. You know stuff like talking about the weather, the birthday boy, where you live, etc. Let's just say by the end of this event, I was wishing I had lied about all my details.

As we were loading all the little children into the train cars for the adventure of a lifetime, I had no idea what lied just five short minutes ahead. Our first stop was across the road in the new barn field. I call it that because this field just got an awesome new barn. The pasture is full of sheep, goats, cows, pigs, and one giant emu bird. It is here where I was given the task of keeping the big bird from taking the pieces of bread out of the little ones' hands. "Hey, Vicki, you take the big bird," Cousin Cindy yelled as she was passing out bread to feed all the animals. *Wait, what?*

For the next twenty or so minutes, I danced around the field with a long-legged bird. I would toss little pieces of bread this way and that way, slowly walking that creature away from all the happy children. There were a few times, I thought, I actually heard dueling Western music while we stared each other down. Big bird wanted to join the party, and I wanted him not to. I had one job at this shindig, and I intended on not failing at it. Then it happened—I ran out of bread. It was tempting to snatch a big piece of Sunbeam out of one of the kiddo's hands, but I didn't. When you are looking eye to eye with a six-foot-tall bird that wanted more bread and you don't have any, thoughts happen. What was I to do now—grab it by the neck and take it down? Ride it off into the sunset?

I intended on being inconspicuous as I walked back through the crowd to the buggy for more bread. Only problem with my plan was the big bird was fast on my heels. Let's just say I didn't walk a straight line either. If he was going to be pecking the back of my head, he was going to have to work for it. No, sir, I was not going to be an easy target for his prehistoric beak. I did everything but stop, drop, and roll to stay out of the line of fire.

As the party was winding down, the main man and I began a conversation with the birthday boy's father. I regret this tremendously for now he knows where we live. It was here we learned he has friends who live in my subdivision next to my sister. Let me set the stage for you. We are on the carport—birthday party winding down; kids, parents, grandparents, aunts, and uncles saying their goodbyes. That man my cousin married is folding up one of the picnic tables. The birthday boy's father is graciously helping with the task. Are y'all with me so far? Cousin Cindy and I make a beeline to help the main man with his table, but seconds before we reach him, it happened. It was one of those moments if you had captured it on a video camera, you would be rich. As my husband slowly turned his picnic table over, he somehow lost his balance and stepped onto the center of the upside down table. What happened next is kind of hard to explain. The force of him stepping on the table slams it to the ground, and since he was still holding tightly to the metal table legs, the downward force catapults him into the air. Y'all, he went to flying like Superman, only without a cape. I kid you not. Want to know what happened next? Well, I'll tell you. On that side of the carport is a big hill that leads down to a barn. He went flying downhill like a fast-pitched baseball being thrown out of the pitcher's hand. About halfway down gravity set in and he hit the ground hard. You would think that would be the end of this embarrassing chaos, but no. He rolled, head over heels like a little girl turning cartwheels. The last part of this gymnastic routine ended up looking like a giant pine tree being rolled into a sawmill.

All we could do was stand there, watching. I thought he never would stop rolling down the hill. I will say once he reached the bottom, he took it like a man—he blamed me. "Why did you push me down the hill?" That was all it took for everyone to burst out laughing. And laughing we did—for hours on end.

I apologized for all the chunks of grass torn slam out of the ground. I will say this, if you can't laugh while hanging with us, then you don't know how to laugh. I just wish those folks didn't know where we lived now. If you hear rumors around town of two folks looking like they were drinking on the job, just nod your head and agree. I'd rather blame this day on alcohol than to say it is just normal behavior for us.

10

The Teacher

In honor of Teacher Appreciation Week, I wanted to let you all know exactly what the word *teacher* actually means. From the outside looking in, most would say it is a person that helps you learn—from your ABCs and 123s, to algebra and English literature and everything in between those things. Well, sit down and let me tell you what it looks like on the inside looking out. My daughter has been teaching since she was three years old. Only I believe her preschool teacher at Temple Baptist Church called it something different. "Goodness, she is a little motherly, isn't she?" Yes, her teacher was correct as was evident by how my toddler had lined all the other preschoolers up to watch her make dinner on the little kitchen in the play area. In fact, she was "in charge" of making sure her older brother did his homework too, whether he wanted the help or not. "Mom, she's bossing me again." He would complain.

It was no surprise to us at all when she declared her college major to be education. All the way through school, she volunteered to teach every opportunity she could—big sister programs, Vacation Bible Schools, day cares, after-school programs, YMCA, and the list goes on and on. She could not wait to be a teacher. The years flew by for us watching a teacher-in-the-making. Fast forward to the last semester—her final student teaching class. She was ready. She marched into that school dressed for success—stylish new bag full of all the necessary supplies to change the world—one student at a time. To this day, I remember her busting through the front door, declaring, "Mom, I need teacher clothes!" Off to the mall we went. With every outfit she tried on, she would ask, "Does this look like a teacher? A real teacher?" She did.

Student teaching was a success until the first day she was unofficially in charge of the classroom—her mentor teacher was sick—and this day was forever to be known as the longest day ever in the history of classroom teaching. There was a substitute teacher called in, but, "I got this," the confident teacher-to-be declared. With her new teacher outfit on and her hair looking like a million bucks, she stood and waited patiently at the door of *her* classroom as the children entered the school. Little children were not the only folks coming down the hallway. She watched with eyes wide open as one very angry mom stomped past the other teachers and headed her way. *Oh, I hope that is not one of my kid's moms,* she thought. But it was.

Not long after the not-so-pleasant encounter with what my daughter called a six-foot-tall angry mom did the day go from bad to worse—the fire alarm. Nothing like being in charge of twenty-five panicking seven-year-olds when you think the school is on fire. "We are gonna die!" the little ones all screamed. As she herded them outside, she noticed all the *real* teachers had green signs in their hands notifying the principal that everyone in their class was safe. He slowly made the rounds inspecting the fast action in removing the children from potential harm. He stopped in front of one embarrassed twenty-two-year-old, as one of her students yelled, "Miss Baylis forgot the sign." I believe if it had only been legal, she would have thumped that precious tattletale in the head. "Oh my gosh, Mom, I gave that man a thumbs-up and a smile. I'm never going to be hired now."

By the end of the day, her feet were swollen, her voice had long been gone, and her hair was now unmanageable. Feeling defeated, she laid her head down on the desk and watched as all the *real* teachers slowly passed her door as if they were checking in on a sick animal at the zoo. By the time she made it home that day, she was in desperate need of a hug. "Is it too late to change my major, Mom? Teaching school is not for me."

Less than a month later, she found herself to be the newest first grade teacher at a local school. It took everyone she knew to help get her very first classroom set up like she wanted—the paint, the curtains, the cute decorations, the rugs, the pictures, the clock, the lamps, the books, the shelves, the beanbags, the tape, the scissors, the crayons, and so on. More than once did her daddy and I get the teacher look when we didn't do something just right. I will admit it, our behinds were dragging at the end of every day, hers too. It takes many an hour and many a day to set a classroom up—something I never knew from the outside looking in.

Over the course of the last couple of years, I have seen this young teacher give up her own grocery money to buy boxes and boxes of Little Debbie snack cakes. I will never forget the first time I saw her putting them in her grocery buggy. "I've got kids that don't have much to eat on the weekends. I put them in their backpacks," she whispered. When you see a teacher standing at the end of a lunchroom table yelling at her children to eat—there may be a reason the rest of us don't see—don't judge them. And remember some teachers just spent their own lunch break opening twenty-five packs of ketchup and milk cartons until your child learns how to do it for themselves. A teacher carries burdens of knowing things like who is hungry and things far worse. At the end of every day, as *her* children walk out from the safety of her room, she knows what some of them may be going home to—sometimes, it is to a world that the rest of us can't handle.

It has been an honor to see this side of what a teacher looks like. Only a teacher will wear a pirate costume out the front door of the house if it will encourage kids to learn. She will grow beans in Styrofoam cups knowing good and well that she will spend an hour mopping the floor after the planting is done. It is a teacher that makes sure mothers will get at least one Mother's Day card. A teacher will introduce your kids to pumpkin pie when they are learning about Thanksgiving and to root beer floats when they are learning about science experiments. She will check your kids for lice—and herself too. She will receive many a marriage proposal from little boys, and she will put many a bow back in your little girl's hair when it falls out.

She will try her best to make a paycheck stretch far enough to make sure all the children in her classroom can go on the field trip. She will beg for volunteers. Her bulletin board will be decorated hundreds of times. She will spend endless hours searching the web for awesome ideas to teach your kids about farm animals and spelling words and math problems. She will laugh at all your kid's jokes. She will read them books. She will grade papers and grade papers and grade papers.

At the end of the day, she will pick her head up off the table, wipe the dust off her hands, and get her classroom ready for the next day. On the outside, she may be five foot two if you stretch her neck, but on the inside, she is tough as nails—she has to be—she's a teacher.

11

Easter

I, Vicki Baylis, do hereby confess the following sin: I forgot to take an Easter family picture.

In lieu of said photo, I submit the following picture through words. I wore blue capris and a blue-and-white top. I love the color blue, but in all honesty, it was about the only thing that fit. The shoes were comfortable but old and not really in fashion. My hair was pinned up in a clip because I was cooking the Sunday meal. There was no jewelry. I wore light makeup—may have actually forgotten to put mascara on. The main man wore khakis with a tan fishing shirt and flip-flops—I pick my battles—flip-flops is not one of them. Although his hair needs cutting again, he was quite handsome.

The oldest child would have been the tallest in the picture—if I had actually taken one. He was dressed, but I can't remember what he was wearing because I was busy cooking. His beard is still there, covering up his beautiful face. The youngest child, my daughter, was as cute as ever, just late. If I had actually taken the picture, we would have been standing out in the yard by the beautiful lake, waiting on her to show up.

Her boyfriend, Nathan, would have been in the picture too. No idea what he was wearing, but they are a real cute couple. He really enjoyed the meal. Sadly, Eli's girlfriend was sick, and if we had taken a picture by the beautiful lake, she would have been in there looking just as cute as ever.

So there you have it. I may have forgotten to take the photo by the lake, but I didn't forget the meaning for the day. He is my Savior, and He is risen. Happy Easter 2015.

12

My Cattle Brokering Days

And the next thing I knew, I was standing in a field of longhorns and Watusi cows—scared. I was scared to death. Let me back up to the beginning. It all started out so innocently I tell you—innocently. My friend had bought a new under-the-counter ice machine, and she wanted Chris to install it. Truly not a big deal at all for the main man, one plug and one waterline. As you all may recall, I ride with him sometimes on his service calls. Everyone calls me the boss—he laughs—but I'm there to mostly talk to the customers, because quite frankly, it's what I do best. Anyway, as the main man was working, we got to talking about barns and land and cows—cows, you say? Yep, it turns out this family wanted some longhorn cattle to put at their new place. I just so happened to know someone that was getting out of the longhorn cattle business. Ta-da! And with these few words, I instantly became a cattle broker. "Hey, my Uncle Charles is selling his longhorns."

So as we wrapped up our short visit at this man's house, plans were made. And as I said while ago, the next thing I knew, I was standing in a field of green grass with the biggest longhorn cattle ever. And the man wanting the cattle was walking the fields with my kinfolk, picking out cows. "I'll take this one and that pair over there." I could hear him say to my cousin Charles Albert. Those men walked and talked about cattle for a good while. I, on the other hand, was over by the Kubota side by side keeping far enough distance away from those horns. "Oh, boy, um, Cindy, make that thing stop coming toward me."

There were a couple of things Cindy and I noticed right off the bat about the difference in this man's buying technique and ours. For starters, he wasn't turning the price tags over and yelling, "Oh my stars! Does this price include a new car or something?" Not once did he have to ask the sales clerk, "Where's your clearance section?" I'll admit, if it had been me standing out there in that field of cows, I would be looking for the ones with a scratch or a dent. Now I say all that not to make this couple look bad—no, sir—because I know too much is giving, much is expected. And this couple, no doubt, lives by that saying. They walk the walk and talk the talk. They were the nicest, friendliest couple I've ever met.

Even Cousin Cindy decided she would sell her Watusi bull and Watusi momma cow. Those things were beautiful as far as cows go, that is. Quite frankly, I don't know how those creatures hold their heads up with those giant horns, but they do. After the shopping was done, it was time to load them up. By "load up," I mean take those free-roaming longhorn cattle out of the green pastures and put them on a trailer. That should be fun, right?

It took two trucks with two big trailers to get all those beauties hauled off. Charles Albert did most of the work, being that he is a cattle whisperer. I kid you not. It is safe to say I watched from a distance. Every once in a while, my cousin would yell over to us, "Okay, nobody move." He walked around those cows a few times, and soon, one by one, those things just walked onto the cattle trailers—just walked onto the trailer. I tell you it was the craziest thing I have ever seen. Now that is not to say that once they got on that cattle trailer, they didn't fight each other for the best seat because they did that all right.

After the first trailer was filled to the max, Uncle Charles and my hubby took off down the road. All we onlookers moved the four-wheelers and the Kubota side by side to another field. Soon enough, those cows and the Watusi bull walked onto the second trailer, and we headed down the road to their new home.

Of course, I should say it takes some skill to haul cattle, especially the kind with horns a mile long. Every once in a while, one of those horns would stick out the side of the cattle trailer, and I would pray they wouldn't take out a stop sign or a pedestrian along the way. I'm not going to mention what those horns can do to a fabric-covered tops either. I know it was probably a little sad for my Uncle Charles because these cows were his pride and joy. They were well cared for and loved. Each one of them had some history—when they were born, how many babies they had had, where he bought them, and on and on. My uncle watched these animals from his porch for years on end, and now they were gone. When your pets, even those that weigh thousands of pounds, are loved like family, you can't help but to worry about them—will they be cared for in the same way? Well, as we pulled in to their new home, I can only imagine what those creatures were saying to each other. "Well, will you lookee there." One by one, they stepped off the trailer and into the magical land of plenty—all fourteen hundred acres of green pastures. Yep, Ole Betsy and Daisy were going to be living the dream.

I have to admit, the cows weren't the only ones with their mouths opened wide catching flies. "Is that a helicopter pad?" Cindy asked. It was. Dang, we wanna live here too. Chances are, it's going to take one of those helicopters to find them cows now. I'm sure no one is ever going to get those things back on a trailer for they are living the grazing dream for sure.

Even my Uncle Charles could not be sad anymore. When we pulled out of there, he said, "Vicki, y'all find us a steak house for supper." This brokering job paid out all right. He treated us to White Caps on the coast. Can't beat that pay for nothing. But most of all, no amount of money can buy the laughter and family memories we experienced along the way that day. "Hey, Cindy, I think one of us stepped in something bad because this truck sure is stinking." But we didn't care, for it was worth it all. Love my Uncle Charles and my family—good people, real good people.

13

Mother's Day 2015

Well, ladies, today is *the* day. You know the day set aside for us to have breakfast in bed, Mother's Day cards, and a gift or two. Yes, ma'am, it is our day. It doesn't matter how old we are either—we are getting hugs today. Usually, when a special day like this is approaching, I start thinking about what to write, and this story was no exception. I asked my friends to recall characteristics of mothers from their childhood versus mothers of today. Some of the things mentioned were things I remembered too. Raise your hand if you have ever gotten a spanking from someone else's mother? A mother of two little boys said that today's mothers have more fear—I agree. This world is a lot more troubled than when we were growing up. The scariest thing I remember was having to check the candy in my Halloween bag.

Today's mothering is certainly different. Who can remember "the look?" Raise your hand if you ever got a case of the sassy mouth during your teenage years. Now raise your hand if your mother knew how to fix that illness. Boom, just like that—cured. My favorite thing today is suppertime. How many of you ever had your mother stand at the table and take your order? Not me! There was one meal and one meal only. It was not Cracker Barrel at our house.

All this thinking about the differences between the mothers, then and now, I am going to blame on *Mad Men*. It is the greatest television series in the history of this planet. In case there is the slightest chance of someone other than myself not knowing about Netflix, let me be the first to welcome you to this century. You know what else I discovered on Netflix? *Mad Men*, episode 1. If you are not careful, you will find something else too—the end of the Internet. That's right—the end. Before I got to the last episode, my Internet cable provider was notifying me that I had reached the end. Wait, what? Apparently, you are only allotted a certain amount of the World Wide Web per month, and if you reach it, they will call. The next thing I knew, I was explaining my addiction to Netflix and asking for a sponsor.

Anyway, back to my Mother's Day story. Mothers back then—in the era of *Mad Men*—had the upper hand, and everyone knew it. I am not sure when some of our mothers gave up this power. If you picked up some of the kids today and placed them in our mother's house back then, there wouldn't be a peach tree limb left on this earth.

Mothers need to get that power back, and let me tell you why. Evil has taken over. First, I am about to jump on my soapbox, and I know there will be folks who will strongly disagree with me. As my daughter used to say, when she didn't want anyone telling her what to do, "Keep your seat. I got this." Yesterday was a horrible day in the city of Hattiesburg. We lost two of our officers. When I say "our" officers, I mean "ours." It has sent our little community into a world of sadness—a gut-wrenching kind of sadness.

There is no way we could celebrate this day knowing a couple of mothers across town were suffering the worst kind of sadness. We could feel their tears. There is an eerie quietness that has fallen over us. They were part of us—our extended family. There may be a lot of things that we do wrong here in the South, but loving our community is not one of them.

Tonight, there will be a candlelight vigil and tomorrow a memorial service. We will walk hand in hand to honor these two men. Honestly, it has taken me all night and all day to not hate those who choose an evil path, and truthfully, I am still working on it.

In fact, I was sitting in church—working up a good mad—when lo and behold that preacher man brought God into this terrible, terrible event. I can't speak for every church service happening in this town today, but I know for a fact that God spoke through our preacher this morning. He did not point fingers at anyone or pass judgment on those who choose the wrong path. Instead, he said we as believers in Christ need to be the thermostat and not the thermometer. We as a people need to be a safe place in our community during this time of heartbreak. Let us be the voice of reason and the hands and feet of Jesus.

He also said we may have trouble finding our quiet time with God because of this terrible tragedy. He is right. We need to drop to our knees and pray for our community. Pray for those who are choosing the wrong paths. Pray that evil will leave our town alone. Pray for our children. Pray for our citizens. And pray for the officers and emergency personnel who called these two men brothers. Those who may be having trouble bending that knee—like me—because of anger, remember this: today, on this day, there are two mothers who did not get that hug.

14

The Untitled One

There are good days and bad days. And then there are days like today—there is no name for days like today. I didn't put a title on this short story because I can't think of an appropriate one. Somehow, the title "Today, I Screamed in the Doctor's Office" just doesn't do it justice. If you have been following my journey for any length of time, then you know I injured my knee when I fell into that stupid pothole in a parking lot. Then to make matters worse, I slid down a fireman's pole—had to—everybody else was doing it. Then fast forward to today, my return visit to the doctor.

First, let me fill in the gap from the fireman pole to now. Yes, I take full credit for my actions. I blame it on pride. You see, my husband, my cousin Cindy, and that man she married all slid down the pole. I could not be the only one to not do it. I literally walked up and back down those stairs twenty times. Each time defeated by that stupid pole. But on that twenty-first time, I did it. So in defense of the fireman's pole, it was the stairs that took the toll on my knee—the pole actually turned out to be easy.

Anyway, ever since then, I have hobbled and moaned and groaned. Again, it was my fault. My whole life now revolves around my knee. "How are you feeling today, knee? You think today we can actually do a little something?" The day I found myself sitting on one of the benches in Walmart thinking about carjacking someone's motor scooter, I realized I have reached rock bottom. I was on a bench in Walmart—you know, where the old people sit when they get tired.

I took so much Tylenol and Advil that my labs were all out of whack. Awesome—I've killed my liver. Stupid pothole. Of course, the recheck labs were fine, and all is well with the organs, except maybe my brain—jury is still out on that. And that gets me back to today, my doctor's visit.

Y'all, he is just awesome, and his staff is super great. If you recall, I had an injection in my knee a few months back and I wanted another one because it worked great! Since I have been having great pains in my knee, he ordered some x-rays. No problem because I really needed to redeem myself in the x-ray department anyway. Big sigh here because what I'm about to say is hard to admit. By the way, if you are a man, it is best you stop reading now. It will save both of us tons of embarrassment.

Here is what happened at the last visit. Women already know this, but if you are a man and still reading this, please know they always asked about "girl things" and they always need a date to put on their stupid charts. If you can't remember the date of certain "girl things," they will send you down the hall to the lab with a little cup. Insert embarrassed fifty-year-old hobbling down the hallway holding that cup. I was never so happy to hear I was not pregnant—they probably were too. Today, I happily reported a date so she could put on that chart—lesson learned the hard way.

Now to the part of the story where I screamed in the doctor's office. I guess my knee was extremely sensitive to the needle—that or my doctor suddenly hates me. "You certainly are my loudest patient," he said. With all my screaming, I may have inadvertently "healed" a few sick folks who were waiting to be seen—you are welcome. There may have been a few cancelations. Again, you are welcome—hope you enjoyed your shift ending early this afternoon.

15

No Good Deed

I tell you this story, not as a way of bragging because we all got things we do and we all got things that we should be doing. But I got this group of friends—a really good group. First, let me explain the dynamics of my list of Facebook friends. They can be broken down into several categories. The outer circle I describe as those who don't live in my town. These folks give thanks daily that they can and do use the excuse, "Oh, I would help, but I live a few hundreds of miles away." Then there are the others, "I just checked Facebook—don't answer the phone—Vicki's calling." These are my smart friends, although they will help me no matter what when it is important. Next, I got my inner circle. You can easily identify them because they are usually walking around in utter disbelief. "Oh, man, I fell for it again."

It is this group I want to talk about. Facebook is an awesome place if you have an idea and need a few folks to help carry it out. I am the *idea* kind of girl. A fund-raiser, a surprise birthday party, a rally, and a cookout are just a few things I see every day being organized on this social media. Even before the invention of the Internet, there were ways of asking for help, and there were always folks willing to do so.

Take for instance the old coffee ministry at the church. Every Sunday morning, a couple of men would take turns making coffee for the members. I can still see my husband lining up the coffee filters, filling up the insulated carafes and wheeling them out to specific areas of the church: the lobby, the senior adults area, and the children entrance. It was a real easy ministry—about six pots of coffee. To this day, my friend Kinslow has never let me forget that I asked him to help take a Sunday turn with this *easy* ministry. In my defense, I had no idea the coffee ministry would blossom into a twenty-eight-pot coffee ordeal every Sunday morning, not just regular and decaf coffee either. It began to take on a Starbucks atmosphere. I still giggle a little at the thought of Kinslow pushing that cart of carafes through our church. Even my husband was giving me the stink eye. "I'm breaking a sweat, Vicki." He would say as he strolled that cart by me.

When time came to gather up volunteers for breakfast at the homeless shelter, I knew just who to call. I needed oranges, scrambled eggs, donuts, and paper products. Kinslow had long since wised up—he chose all things paper; I think he is still having coffee flashbacks to this day. It looked like my friend Kat had taken a fast-flying trip down to Florida and shook a few trees before she got her car unloaded. It took her forever to slice oranges. Surprisingly, she volunteered for the paper products the next time around. I felt bad for the rest of Hattiesburg when Phillip and his wife started bringing in the boxes of donuts. I will tell you this, it ain't easy asking someone to scramble twelve dozen eggs for a crowd. "Say what? I don't have that many chickens," said Cousin Cindy. We were worn out by the time that breakfast was over. You wanna know what happened next? We all volunteered to do it all over again.

Now I say all that to bring up the day someone had the idea of feeding the lawmen. It was a great idea, and of course, we all wanted to help. "Shoot yeah!" If you ever get a hankering to volunteer, let me go ahead and tell you who always shows up—karma. Yep, every time. Like when you spend an hour loading up the car only to have it not start back up again. Then when you finally find the jumper cables and get going, "Don't turn this car off until you get there, Vicki." Only you forget and turn the car off two miles down the road. Or when you see Phillip dragging a six-foot cooler across the parking lot because you asked him to bring the ice. Or afterward, when every time you give someone a ride, they ask, "What's that smell in your car?" And you have to tell them about the time the gigantic Crock-

Pot of green beans spilled out. Yep—karma. But you know what happens next? My friends will volunteer all over again.

I want to give special thanks to our chef Amanda for making enough spaghetti to feed an army. Joy and Rita were my bread girls this time around. To everyone who made salads and desserts, you are awesome. Angi with Gourmet & More never complained when I would call and ask her to add another platter of this or that. To my friends—Katrina, Cathy, Tina, Kat, Leany, Terri, and Kim—we could not have done it without your help. And finally to Kinslow, Phillip, and Chris, you guys rock. I think I heard Phillip was selling his ice chest—not sure why.

16

I Heard About It on Facebook

So it must be true, right? Because we all know that the best medical and legal advice comes from our news feed. This morning was the perfect example of how I am reminded that we are not actually in charge of our own self. As you may recall, I fell into a parking lot hole last month and injured my knee. Of course, I went to the doctor and got steroids and pain pills. No big deal. Since my knee was not healed when I went for my follow-up visit, they ordered an MRI. Hopefully, I can get that done this week—waiting on payday, you know?

Now I say all that to say this. The main man has been having knee pains too. It never fails. Whatever one of us has, the other one feels it too. Anyway, I saw on Facebook someone posting about an over-the-counter pain pill. It is supposed to do wonders for body aches according to my Facebook source. Since we all know I have a zero tolerance for pain, I am going to give it a try.

At five minutes until closing time last night, I wheeled our crippled bodies into the local pharmacy and purchased a bottle of this miracle drug. Like a couple of drug addicts, we popped two each into our mouths. Ta-da! We are going to be cured. Let me tell you what happened next. Either I was extremely worn out and did not know it, or those two pills had some sort of magic sleeping ingredients in them that knocked me out—out cold. While I was snoring away in my bed, the main man's head was itching up a storm—a fact I am mentioning now but he did not bother to relay to me until the next morning.

As I am getting ready for church, I noticed something about my husband. "What did you do?" Welts all over the side of his face. He had popped two more of those magic pills to get ahead of his knee pains. Back to the pharmacy we run—no Benadryl in my house.

Let's just say the main man is not a happy patient right now. It's not because he was already dressed for church and I made the call to stay at home and watch it on the Internet either. I didn't want the preacher's sermon to be drowned out when the snoring started once his Benadryl kicked in. Even though he is ill as a hornet that I got my medical advice from Facebook, that is not the main reason he is not talking to me. Nope, not the reason. It's not because the side of his face has welts all over it either or the fact his whole body is itching from top to bottom. It's because he is more than likely going to be passed slam out when the Saints kickoff at noon. "If I miss this game, I will be mad," said my "who dat" fan as he was trying desperately to keep his eyelids open. He would have been better off with the knee pain.

17

Code Drama, Room 2

It is safe to say I don't handle pain well. Never have, never will. Zero pain tolerance. I admit this. It is more than likely written in big red letters on my medical chart down there at the clinic. You may remember my saying that I fell in a hole in a parking lot. If you didn't hear about that, I don't know how you missed that big news because I have complained about it for months. I still have a little pain with it too. Not enough to take my emergency pain pill and certainly not enough to have surgery. Nonetheless, I still have a little pain, hence, the reason my doctor gave me a few emergency pain pills.

I tell you that to tell you this. I hurt my back. I don't know how. It started with what I called a little sting. I found myself asking my husband, "Come look. I think something has bitten me." He would look and find nothing. This mysterious pain rocked on for a week. "Come look now." I would say. Yet again, he would not see anything. A few days later, the sting turned into a burning sensation. "Come look now, Chris. I think I am on fire." Still, he reported seeing nothing. Then a day later, the stinging and the burning turned into pressure, like someone was standing on my back. I just could not stretch it out.

Finally, this mysterious back problem turned into pain. Whoa, stop the world. I don't do pain. Enough pain that I reached into my bottle of emergency pain pills and took a half of one. I guess the pain went away, because the next morning, I woke up. Let me tell you what I did next. I consulted all my Facebook friends. Folks, under no circumstances do I recommend this ever. Why didn't I learn my lesson the last time I sought medical advice? One by one, the medical diagnoses came in. Afterward, I was scared to sleep without the lights on. According to them, I was having a heart attack along with a case of the shingles. I went to bed taking another half a pain pill and an aspirin, in case the heart attack part was right.

The next day, I called the clinic—I had to. I was not about to use any more of my emergency pain pills designated for my knee on my failing heart. Of course, my doctor, the one who knows all about me and my crazy body, was busy. "I can get you in with someone else. Will that be okay?" Well, shoot yeah, my heart is on its last leg, and I got shingles.

After a few pleasantries between us and a brief explanation of my symptoms, this sweet lady dressed in a white lab jacket took a look. And by "look," I mean I believe she shot me with a Taser gun while my back was turned. Sweet stars, this woman is evil. I have no idea how she knew the exact spot that would send me off that table, but she did. Into the x-ray room I go. It didn't take her long to figure out I needed steroids and muscle relaxers. Then she said, "You can take a whole pain pill, you know?" You want to know what I did next? Nothing! Folks, I lost three whole days of my life. As much as I do not like to hurt, I cannot be in a drug-induced coma, and I tossed those pain pills back in the cabinet.

In my brilliance, I decided I must be healed—no more pain. I totally regret what I did next. I rode with my husband to a customer's house. Before I go any further, let me explain this. I do love dogs. They are awesome. But it is summertime in Mississippi. It is hot, and I was sticky as I watched my husband work from the comfort of a lawn chair. And then it happened. And by "it," I mean those big slobbery dogs preceded to bathe me, like a pup, with their tongues. Take me home, Jesus, take me home. I tell you this because it will be very important info in a few minutes.

The next day, I decided not to venture out on service calls—it was my turn to accompany Mother to her doctor's appointment. As I was getting ready, I noticed the most horrible thing imaginable—I had a tick. Yes, a tick on my body. Thank you, dogs. The good news is the clinic can work me in within fifteen minutes. Guess who had an opening? The woman with the Taser gun. But I didn't care. Having a tick stuck on your body will cause you to do things you would not normally do, like not wear a bra in public. Yes, I did say that out loud. I could not put my bra on because I was actually scared it would rip the tick body off me leaving the nasty head stuck inside.

Folks, you want to know what will cause you to lose all dignity? Tell the front desk you have a tick stuck on you. Next, sit in a crowded waiting room without a bra on. Then have a total stranger walk over to talk about Jesus. Apparently, I looked like I might have needed a little Jesus. No dignity left.

A few minutes later, I was de-ticked and headed out the door. As much fun as the body search for ticks was, it was nothing compared to what happened next. Two hours after I took my first dose of that antibiotic, I found myself asking, "Hand me that medicine bottle." Sweet stars! What meth house lab did they get this stuff from? I feel like I have come down with the flu. My throat hurts, and my tongue is sore. Apparently, to remove tick germs from your body, you need to swallow nuclear chemicals. I think I stand a better chance with the tick. I told my husband if I pass out, make sure 911 checks to see if my tongue is still there.

18

Getting Old Is Not for Sissies

You know those very big bouncy exercise balls you find in fitness gyms everywhere? I think they do some kind of yoga on them. If you know anything about me, then you know that information is strictly hearsay. I'll get back to this shortly, but first, I want to remind you that my back is still hurting. Seriously, I have become the old lady who is constantly talking about her ailments. My husband is the same way. When did we turn into old people? We walk around moaning and groaning all the time.

I consider myself somewhat smart, well, at least a little above average at times. So yesterday, while I was changing the bed linens, I had an epiphany—is that the correct word? It was more like an aha moment—our moans and groans must be caused by our old mattress. Years ago, we purchased one of those pillow-top mattresses. Honestly, it has been good to us over the years, but alas, it is now old and worn out. If you guys are anything like us, a new mattress is not in the budget at the moment, so in all my genius, I yelled for the main man to come help me turn this mattress over. He did. Of course, it took everything we had to flip that thing over without breaking lamps, laptops, and picture frames. Ta-da! I have fixed all our moans and groans.

After I got the clean sheets on the bed, we both jump on to check out our "new" mattress. It was hard as a rock. Yep, like a giant slab of concrete. The pillow top that is now the bottom of this mattress made us feel as if we were lying on top of one of those big bouncy exercise balls. But the bed was already made, so it shall remain. Besides, my husband liked it.

Fast forward to bedtime. Within seconds, the main man was out like a light and snoring. I, on the other hand, was having trouble getting comfortable. Seriously, it was as if I was sleeping outside on a sidewalk. Everything began to hurt—my elbows, my anklebones, my shoulders, my hips, and let me never forget what this concrete bed was doing to my knees. I blame it on my weight. Everywhere I turned, I was causing pressure points on my body. When I finally got to the point where I convinced myself that I was having trouble breathing, I said, "Wake up! My lungs are deflating." That had to be it. My lungs were in between my weight and the concrete. He was not happy about being summoned to tend to my new medical crisis, and he hastily turned over. This is when I thought the whole mattress—sheets, pillows, and all—was about to slide off to the floor. "Stop moving and let me get off this bed before we kill ourselves."

It is safe to say this idea was a bust, nothing like flipping a mattress back over at midnight. This morning, when my husband got out of bed, he hollered. His hips are out of place, and he can't walk without hurting. I am sore too. Thank goodness, we turned that mattress back over in the nick of time. We feel like we both aged ten years last night. Concrete beds are not for old people. Today, we start saving for new mattresses. Live and learn.

19

What Exactly Is Love?

I remember several years back someone asked the question: "What is love?" Many of the young whippersnappers today go through life with a false definition of what the word actually means—a fairy-tale kind of thing. In fairness, that's what I probably thought too when I was younger. Now that I have been married longer than being single, I can safely say I understand the true meaning. A fairy tale it is not.

First, let me state for the record that love is all rainbows and sunshine—for the first fifteen or so minutes. You notice a stranger across the room, your eyes meet, your heart skips a beat, and your stomach flips like you are on a roller coaster. You can't stand being apart for even a few minutes. Oh, you have met the perfect person. Everything is great; it must be love, right?

Then you get married. As long as the bills are getting paid, the kids are healthy, the kitchen table always has food on it, and the schedules are not too hectic, life is great with this perfect person. You have a roof over your head. The car works like a charm, and the gas tank is on full. Life is wonderful; it must be love, right?

Then reality hits. Believe it or not, that perfect man you could not live without begins to snore. In all honesty, the only reason you have not stopped the loud freight train sleeping next to you with a pillow is the jail time that would surely follow. He is always leaving dirty clothes on the floor and dishes in the sink. Before long, you find yourself looking for the perfect spot to hide his body because you made it perfectly clear that the toilet seat goes down—always down. Yet somehow, during the middle of the night, you fell inside the toilet bowl once again. The bills are backing up. The car won't crank. The lawn mower is broken, and since you didn't get paid, the yard will remain uncut—hopefully next month you can get it fixed. Heaven forbid, the perfect man of yours will actually shut a cabinet door. You find yourself standing in your kitchen, holding onto a cast iron skillet, and saying, "You better make him invisible, God, 'cause I am about to whop him over the head." But you don't, because it must be love, right?

In all fairness to my main man, I will admit I am no longer perfect either. My home-cooked meals have been replaced by ham sandwiches and things from a box. There is always laundry on the end of our bed. I forget more things than I remember. I give new meaning to the words *mood swings*. If you recall, I do complain about something hurting every other week. This month, it is my back. Come to find out that knot I have on my back is probably muscles that are pumped up like a Mr. Universe man. You want to know why? It's not because I work out either. Come to find out there is a medical term for the fact I have a big butt and those muscles are just tired of toting it. While I am at it, let me tell you what happens when you accidentally take your muscle relaxant twice. You will find yourself sliding out of your car and your husband saying, "If you are going to be a pillhead, you are going to have to start writing this stuff down." We, and by we, I mean him, liked to have not got me up our stairs. I would have enjoyed my state of "high," but I was too busy making peace with my maker. "Lord, Jesus, don't let me do this again." Yep, I am not what I used to be, but he still keeps me around. It must be love, right?

Today makes twenty-eight years since we said, "I do." To all you young whippersnappers, cherish the easy years and hang tough through the hard ones. It's certainly not a fairy tale, but it is so worth telling about in the years to come. Happy twenty-eighth anniversary, Chris Baylis. I love you more today than ever before. It must be love, right?

20

So I Went to the Store to Get Eggs

First, let me ask this: do you know what fencing is? You know, the sport with the swords. Well, keep that in mind. Yesterday, I decided to make a home-cooked meal, and I sent the customary text out to my kids—brown sugared, bacon-wrapped pork tenderloin, twice-baked potatoes, green beans, and biscuits. For dessert, I was going to make a lemon pound cake. The lemon pound cake is the reason I needed more eggs. Keep in mind, it is sprinkling pretty heavy outside, but that is really no big deal because I keep an umbrella in my car.

I don't know about y'all, but when we go to the store, we call Mother and ask, "I'm at the store, need anything?" Only on this trip, Mother's cell phone goes straight to voice mail. Hmm. After about thirty minutes of calling Mother's cell phone, I get a little worried. I do what I always do: call my sister Terri. I only call Brother Bill if it's serious—no need to alarm everyone just yet, you know?

"I think she had lab work early this morning. Let me know if you find her," Terri said. After checking out at the grocery store, I head to Mother's house. If you remember, Mother is a diabetic, and sometimes, her blood sugar may drop too low. I do the peep through the glass front door—no lights on. I use my spare key—you know the one I keep because squirrels keep getting Mother's keys? If you have followed my stories for any length of time, then you know what that is all about. I ease through the house flipping lights on as I go, calling her name out all the way. It's when I get to the door of her room, my heart stops. She's in the bed—completely covered head

60

to toe. I can't describe how time literally went into slow motion as I walked over to her bed and eased the covers back. I tell you all, it was the most sickening feeling I have ever had. Never was I so glad to see wrinkled up bed linens and a pillow under that comforter. "Thank you, Jesus. Praise the Lord." Please don't ever tell Mother that I let you know her bed was unmade. It was one of her rules growing up: make your bed.

I check the garage for the car—it's gone. "Well, Terri, she is not at home. I'm headed over to your house now." Mother loves to go to Terri's to see the grandkids before they leave for school. Later in the day, I get to hear her talk about how Rylan was dressed so cute, or how Arabella didn't like her hair, or who has what sporting event or major test that day. She loves those grandbabies, no doubt.

Now bring back to your mind—fencing and the fact it is raining. My sister has about six dogs at her house. Remember, she has five kids, and each one has a dog. Every time I pull in her driveway, I think I am fixing to lose a tire or a bumper. Let's just say those dogs love protecting their house. I know for a fact one of those precious darlings will bite—only I can't remember which one it is.

Sure enough, Mother's car is there, but I find the driver's side passenger door in her van is open, and it is raining. Hmm. There is no way around the fact that I must open my car door and pray the dogs remember, "Oh, it is Aunt Vicki." They don't. It is here I must take the umbrella fencing my way into the garage—two steps forward, two steps back, make a circle, and two steps forward and two steps back. Repeat until you make it into the garage, which is where they sleep, nothing like being an unwanted houseguest in their den. I was never so happy to see my mom come out of Terri's house because I'm still dancing with barking dogs.

"Mom, which one of these little (insert your own word here because I can't repeat mine) bites?" I yell to her.

Mother says, and I repeat word for word, "I'm headed to the grocery store, you need anything?" No, I don't. I am soaking wet, surrounded by the enemy, and seriously lacking the fencing skills needed to keep my sister's dogs away.

"What I need is a stiff drink—dang, Mom, I thought you was dead, and I think these dogs are gonna eat me alive."

I turn Mother's cell phone back on and fence my way back to the car. I tell you all, exiting Terri's driveway is more difficult than entering it. Just put your car in neutral and let those precious things push you out into the road. That way, you won't ever be the aunt who ran over one of their dogs. I can hear it now. "Aunt Tish is the favorite aunt. She never ran over our dogs." Well, in my defense, Aunt Tish never has to track down her momma every week to turn her cell phone back on. Terri said, "We probably should put a GPS in Mom's car." I think she may be right.

21

The Mending of a Heart

By now, you all know I grew up in a trailer park—never been ashamed to say it. It certainly made me who I am today. And like many other folks, there is an untold story that lurks in the back of my mind from time to time—a story about my growing up—but this is not the time to tell it. Honestly, there may never be a perfect time either. It seems my heart will not step aside long enough for my hands to write it. I don't dwell on it. It is what it is—an untold story.

Like most everyone else, I finished high school with hopes and dreams of college—a better life, one where the trailer park could be a far distant, forgotten memory. Now don't get me wrong, even though the hardest of times, I was blessed. I know this. After one glorious part-time semester of college, reality set in—there was no money to be found for this dream. It took a toll on my heart. I look back at my first job with the fondest of memories. I was 3T, Vicki, unit clerk at Forrest General Hospital—third floor, tower wing. I still am in my heart, so to speak, because I was a life-sized sponge absorbing all the new stuff around me. I still do that today everywhere I go. It was here that I watched what life outside of the confinements of a trailer park was all about. There were many role models—hardworking men and women—who helped shape what my future was to be.

Dressed in a navy blue uniform, I sat at my desk on 3T. As I write this, I smile at the memory because that uniform was not the loveliest of sights either, but it was perfect to me. From my little desk, I watched everyone as they strolled in and out of the busy nurse's station—each one of them giving me a glimpse into a better life. I could spend many a paragraph talking about everyone who walked past my desk—Angie, Linda, Janet, Vera, Mrs. Jeanne V, Cindy, Katrina, Bettye, Mrs. Davis, and so many more—each having a small part influencing my path. One in particular was a nurse named Mary. Keep in mind, this was back in the day when some of the nurses still wore white hats. I loved Mary's hat, and I wanted it and all that it meant to wear it too—gracefulness, professionalism, a caring heart. Never did I want something as badly as I wanted that hat. Even to the point where I had to refrain myself from asking, "Can I wear your hat?"

I was going to be a nurse—it was the hat—and not just any nurse but the head nurse on 3T, no doubt. After all, how hard could that job be, right? One of the most special things about that floor was the surgeons—Abraham, Clark, Guice, Ross, Whitehead, Aseme, Hatten, Varner, Culpepper to name a few who passed by my desk dropping charts off as they tended to their patients. Each one with all the necessary skills to heal the world.

Of all who passed by, though, there was one I watched the most—Dr. T.E. Ross III. I can still hear his voice as he called the floor asking me to gather up the charts needed for making rounds. His strength, his knowledge, his fearlessness, and his confidence I envied. I wanted to have those qualities too even more than I wanted Mary's hat.

Not ashamed to say, I was saddened each time I dropped out of college because the money was just not there. Three years later, it was time for me to leave my little desk on 3T and move on to bigger things—I wanted to work in dialysis. What better place than there to learn nursing? I remember sharing that dream with Dr. Ross as he walked through the station one day. "Tell them I sent you," he said. And I did.

There were many new challenges faced in this new world, and I loved each and every one of them. I have to say the greatest of these was the day I became certified in hemodialysis. Looking back now, I see it as fate, but as a twenty-year-old, it was what nightmares were made of—Dr. T.E. Ross III and one of his post-op patients. I was about to insert a needle into his fresh-out-of-surgery work of art. Could there be more of a challenge than that? Nope. Unless you have been there, there are no words to actually describe it. You know what I did next? I found my courage, my confidence, and my strength. It was there all along, but it took Dr. Ross and one of his patients to bring it out, for one did not simply mess up his post-op patients and live to tell about. Just like that, a broken heart was mended. It had strength, and it had fearlessness, and it had confidence.

I had the opportunity to bump into Dr. Ross about a year ago. I babbled on like I was still that eighteen-year-old on 3T. I had so much I wanted to say, but mostly, I wanted him to know I did in fact become a nurse. Come to find out nursing was a lot harder than those gals of 3T led me to believe. Mary can keep her hat. I don't want it anymore. To this day, when I am facing a difficult time, I reach deep inside the past and summon up the fearlessness, the confidence, and the strength that I learned from watching him.

The day I heard he had gone to live with our Lord, I cried a little. They were tears of thankfulness for God allowing his path to cross mine. Years ago, Dr. T.E. Ross III helped mend my broken heart; he never knew it. May God comfort his family until they meet again. RIP, Dr. T. E. Ross III.

22

My Day in Second Grade

I was sitting at my desk today, minding my own business, coloring inside the lines and using the scissors like a big girl. You know what happened? The teacher said I was being too slow. What? Excuse me? Insert my head bobbing but not enough to get sent to the principal's office, though. Well, I guess we will work a little faster, but first, I need to run to the teacher's workroom. Yep, didn't take me long to regret the fluid pill I had taken this morning for my blood pressure. I can tell you one thing: teachers cannot take fluid pills. While I made the trip down the hall five times, the teacher did not.

Another thing I did today was I made a lot of new friends; being the new kid in class is a big deal. The teacher had tables set up with all different kinds of things on them to do. Each table brought a new task and an opportunity to learn. Each time the centers changed, I met a whole new group of folks. They were busy as bees. While I remained stuck at the "make a frog hat" table, I secretly cherished the fact I did not have to move. More on that a little later, but first, let me say my new friends were precious. Each one of them was all eager to get to the next table. If I heard it once, I heard it a thousand times. "Mrs. Baylis, our table is not finished yet." Then I would get that look from the teacher again. Precious yes they were, but they were big-time tattletales if you ask me.

Each one of them looked different and had a different personality, so it was real easy to tell them apart. Let me tell you what they all had in common: a big smile when they arrived at my table, a big heart when someone needed to borrow the black or red crayon, or a pair of scissors, or the glue stick, and they also had a genuine willingness to learn about frogs. Those kids were so proud of their frog hats, each hat fitting their own uniqueness. In fact, they wore those things to lunch.

Speaking of lunch, I didn't know coloring could be such a calorie burner—maybe it was the scissors. Who knows? Anyway, as we all walked to the cafeteria, in a single line, no doubt, I was wondering what was on the menu today—that and the fact I wished I had taken another trip to the teacher's workroom—stupid fluid pill. Surprisingly, those folks have figured out how to feed a small city with ease. I give my hats off to whoever made the cheesy chicken rice—not bad. I wish you could have seen the little kids as I was trying to pick a seat. Oh, the smile on the little girl's face when I chose to sit in between her and the teacher—priceless. My favorite part of the cafeteria was when a little kid asked me my name—those young'uns are so welcoming. "Your name is Miss Baylis, and your daughter's name is also Miss Baylis? Why would you name her the same name? That is confusing." These came out of the mouths of children. Loved it.

My favorite part of the day is what I had hoped to call nap time; the kids went to P.E. but nope. Lo and behold, Miss Baylis had a ton of work for me to do. The loud thumping noise you may have heard was when I had to use all my fingers to check math papers. I'm here to tell all the volunteers this: when the coloring is done, leave. Just leave. It was all downhill from there. Somewhere around the last layer of darkness—I mean end of schooltime—my body began to ache, more like revolt. Good stars, second grade is hard. If it had not been rude, I would have raised my hand and told the teacher, "Stop smiling. There is nothing left to smile about." Come to think of it, everyone was smiling—the students, the teachers, the principals, and the cafeteria ladies. What's up with that? I needed a nap and a bath, and I wanted to go home but couldn't. The teacher was going to take me home right after her trip to Walmart. There are no words to describe Walmart after a day in second grade—no words.

I tell you all that to tell you this. I have no idea how teachers go home and raise a family—cook supper, clean house, take kids to dance and ball practice, etc. If you know a teacher, tell her she is awesome. Let her know she is appreciated. In fact, bake her a cake. If you think that is not warranted, then come sit with me at the frog hat table tomorrow—don't take your fluid pill. Now if you will excuse me, I'm not finished crying yet, and I need to find someone to rub my feet.

23

Did the Warranty Run Out?

October is my birthday month, and before I dive headfirst into age fifty-one, I want to reflect on my year of being the big five-o. If I had to sum it up in a few words, those words would be *doctor's appointments*. Yep, I spent more time at the clinic than I did at home. Not really, but you should see my clinic bill. Somehow, I managed to have three—count them—MRIs this year. Surprisingly, they all were applied to my deductible, shaking my head in disbelief. There were two injections in my knee, physical therapy—twice, one tick removal. Do I need to mention the hole I fell into in the parking lot? Then there was the brief lapse of judgment when I put on Facebook that I was having a burning feeling in the center of my back. Lesson learned the hard way. I went to bed that night thinking I was in the midst of a heart attack and shingles—none of which I had. Facebook doctors are not real doctors, just so you know.

Before I forget, I want to say a special thank-you to my ortho-pedic doctor and his staff of nurses, including the x-ray tech who insisted I take the walk of shame down to the lab for a pregnancy test at age fifty—age fifty! At the time, I figured that would be my most humiliating event of the year. No, I was wrong. It wasn't. A close second was when I called Jesus to the room to help with my knee injections. Then there was the awesome moment when I learned my big behind was causing my back to ache. Let that sink in, will you?

Needless to say, I am just thankful I survived the year in one piece. If I can give all of you approaching the half-a-century mark any advice, it would be: live life to the fullest now, the warranty runs out at fifty, and Walmart does not carry replacement parts. You will no longer be able to slide down the fireman pole without heading to the doctor, explaining to him why you thought it would be fun is difficult. Another thing you need to know is buy reading glasses in bulk. One day, I was fine, and the next, I was messing up recipes left and right. Is it too much trouble to make the writing bigger on the Duncan Hines box? I think not. You will never remember what you came into a room to get, so don't stress about it. Fluid pills are evil, and you will eventually visit every bathroom in the state of Mississippi whether you want to or not.

Your days of multitasking will become a distant memory. Cleaning the house is a week-long event now. And forget the yard—just let it go. Besides, if you take your reading glasses off, you won't see it anyway, and then chances are you will forget all about it after a few minutes.

Medication will become an issue. You know those cute little pillboxes with the days of the week written on them? Buy one. The side effects from taking your muscle relaxant twice by mistake is far greater embarrassing than buying the stupid pillbox ever could be. Speaking of the muscle relaxants, let me tell you about my back pain. I had succumbed to the fact I would be plagued with a life of back pain forever, but thanks to the good folks at Lake Serene Physical Therapy, I may just very well survive age fifty. One more therapy session left to go. If you happened to go there, tell them I said hello. And if you are tired of hearing about my ailments, stop following now—my colonoscopy and mammogram are already scheduled. Age fifty—a tough one but I survived. I'm looking forward to this next year and hope you will tag along too. Happy Birthday to me!

24

It's Not a Printer, But...

This was not just any old printer either, but a wireless one. Cousin Cindy and that man she married have a top-of-the-line printer—she can print something from her car, in another state, if she wants to do so. It will be sitting there waiting on her when she gets home. And while I am not envious of that printer, I set a goal to have one when the time was right. The main man and I have been skipping on birthdays, anniversaries, and such because we have made it a goal to pay off all our bills and be debt free. This was a slow process, mind you, but one that we will meet hopefully before having to move into the nursing home. Anyway, we keep paying off bills one by one, still have more to do, but we are working hard on them. If we owe you money, just hang tight.

As most of you who follow my chaos already know, I have had the year of medical drama. It seems I met my deductible right off the bat—in January. Since my insurance policy year runs June to June—found that out a few months back—I met my deductible again in July. Kid you not. While I was out doing my part of adding new floors to the local medical community, my husband has not contributed anything. That is not to say he has not been sick, he just has refused to go to the doctor. The main man has been a little under the weather. I finally talked him into a trip to the clinic for his sinuses. It was more like, "If you don't go to the doctor, I will accidentally stop your loud snoring with this pillow while you are sleeping." He went—got antibiotics, steroids, and Sudafed. Then he went again and got some more. On the third trip, a few months later, I didn't want to pick the Sudafed up from the pharmacy. I'm pretty sure he is on some kind of DEA watch list by now. "Tell that doctor you don't want any more Sudafed. I'm not going to jail with you, you hear?"

It was on that third visit I decided to accompany him into the room. I then proceeded to fill the doctor in on all the concerns I am having—rather all the ailments my husband is having. Believe it or not, but the doctor was concerned too. I knew he would be. Test, test, and more tests have followed. Let's just say the main man is not happy. In fact, he is having one of those tests tonight at the outpatient hospital. I can't wait to hear how his night went; I will see him early in the morning. If you hear a loud thump midmorning, that will be me knocking his behind out and dragging him on to the next doctor's appointment. He has already cancelled it four times today. "I'm not going," he said. But he is.

Which leads me to the reason I am writing this story. As I said earlier, I have been dreaming of my new printer. My husband has been dreaming of grills. Our grill died a long while back and was hauled off to the scrapyard. I can say for a fact he has actually touched almost every grill in Hattiesburg by now trying to pick the perfect one. Up until this week, it looked like we would be getting his grill soon. I am letting him go first since I have a printer. Yes, I have a printer—I keep reminding myself that every day. It is old and does not work with my new laptop, but I have found a way around that little problem. I simply download a copy of whatever I need printed onto a flash drive (is that what they are called now?). I take that flash drive over to another laptop—the antique one that does not have Wi-Fi capabilities or the ability to work all the time—and insert the flash drive then print. Ta-da! So yes, I have a printer.

Yesterday, my dryer went out. Over the last few years, we have replaced almost every part it has except the heating element and the timer knob. Lucky for us, those are the two things that went out this week. Actually, the timer knob went out months ago, but I just kept tinkering with it to keep going—you have to get it just right and that dryer will turn on. Of course, it may turn off again in five minutes, and I would try it again, but at least, I am not down at the creek bank washing my clothes with a rock, so I try not to fuss.

Today, I got a new dryer. As I said before, it is not the new Wi-Fi top-of-the-line printer that I wanted, but it will do. It could be worse, the main man's new grill turned out to be a check written to Wesley Hospital instead, so I won't complain. God reminded me that while my dryer stopped and my printer is old and we don't have a grill to cook hamburgers on, I am still blessed beyond what I deserve.

It's a little too quiet here right now if you ask me. Of course, I am busy with all this backed-up dirty laundry. The new dryer doesn't make the clanging noise like the old one did either. Yep, a little too quiet. Y'all keep my main man in your prayers as the doctor gets him back on track.

25

I'm Not a Lemon-Lime Kind of Gal

Let me start by saying I do not like green or yellow Life Savers. I do not eat green or yellow Jell-O or do I drink Sprite or 7Up. Actually, I don't even drink lemonade either. All this info will be needed later on in this story. First, let me tell you about how my husband fell slam apart. If you really know me, then you probably know that that man of mine snores, like a freight train kind of snoring. It is the reason I have to take some sort of over-the-counter sleeping pill at night. Goodness, if a tornado comes through our area, we can't hear it. Of course, the sleeping pill can't be too strong because I still need to be able to turn him over or wake him up if he stops breathing—yep, I have diagnosed him with sleep apnea. I wake him up no less than twenty times a night—every night. "Turn over. Stop snoring." Hence, this is the reason I am never fully rested. He isn't either.

When he started having shortness of breath, I became concerned, but as always, of course, he refused to go to the doctor. So the first chance I got, I tattled on him. If you remember my saying when he had a sinus infection, I went with him when the nurse called him back to the room. Yes, sir, I started at the top of the list with his snoring and ended with his ADD. The doctor had lots to write about that day. I covered everything I wanted fixed. You want to know what all my tattling did? The entire month of December 2015 was one test after another. Needless to say, I will never be allowed to accompany him again when the nurse calls his name. It is also safe to say we have met our deductibles. The doctor just about took all his blood

74

running lab work, and then he ran him through the x-ray machine a time or two. What followed after that was priceless.

Let me start with his snoring. Oh, that is a fine place the doctor has set up for the sleep apnea test. It looks like a fancy hotel room. Honestly, I was more excited about this than he was. I cannot recall the last time I had a good-night's sleep. I packed him a bag of goodies to munch on during the evening, even got him some new pajamas, and off he went. About three hours into the night, they strapped that CPAP machine on him. I can just hear the discussion going on down at the nurse's station. "Lord, have mercy! We are about to lose the dude in room two. He's not going down on my watch. Quick, get him a machine." Yep, I was right—he has sleep apnea. My husband told me the following morning that he felt better than he has in years. Imagine that, not struggling to breathe all night—oxygen is a wonderful thing.

We have had the CPAP machine at our house going on four nights now. It is the best thing since sliced bread. He has so much more energy during the day—a new man. Not to mention I am sleeping soundly too. He feels so much better. In fact, he actually wanted to cancel the heart doctor visit, declaring his heart problems was because of him not breathing well at night. It could be, but we're not canceling that appointment no matter how much he fussed about it.

"Mr. Baylis, I want to do a stress test on you," said the heart doctor. I wish I had taken a photo of the look I got from him when he was told that. It didn't matter; he was still having the test done. There are two things I need to tell you about the stress test. One is on a treadmill, and the other is done in the x-ray department. I remember telling him, "At least you don't have to walk on the treadmill. The one in x-ray sounds easier." It wasn't, at least according to my soon-to-be ex-husband.

If you are a coffee drinker, like he is, the hardest part about this test should be giving up caffeine twenty-four hours prior to it. This was no problem for him—he is a man. And you all know men can do all things. I guess it was a few hours before leaving the house that morning that his headache showed up. As we pulled into the hospital parking lot, the nausea joined the party. Again, I wish I had a photo of the looks I received while we were sitting in the waiting room. Let me describe it the best I can. Picture this: a room full of grown-ups reading magazines, talking quietly among themselves, passing the time away while waiting on their name to be called. There were several elderly men. You can tell they were once in the military—they had that look, a few housewives, a teenager dressed in her school uniform, and me. Sitting next to me was a fifty-five-year-old man who had magically reverted back to the age of eight. You know the little boy that was always hanging out of his seat, slumped down with his shoulders on the seat bottom, not wanting to be there. "Sit up straight, Chris. Everyone is looking at us." Oh, the look was priceless. I think this was when the ADD burst through the doors, because after that, he spent the majority of the time pacing the hallway, glaring at me every time he passed by the windows.

Every thirty minutes, they called his name. The first time was for getting the IV started. The second time was to look at his heart while it was "napping." But on the third time his name was called, Lord, have mercy! When he walked back through that door, I realized I would need to sleep with my eyes open. Apparently, the third trip in is when they find out how fast your heart can drive. Not only had that happened but also he now had hot flashes. It was a life-changing experience. He said it will make you give up steak and baked potatoes for rice cakes and celery. He is a new man now with a new outlook. That was the closest thing to a heart attack that he ever wants to experience. It was time to get healthy. "Take me home," he said. "I need a nap. I am done with all these tests. Done!"

Now I tell you all that to tell you this. Two days after his stress test, I had my first colonoscopy. Granted I really could not afford it now since we had just helped the hospital build a new wing with all his tests, but I had had it scheduled for months. As you all know, when you turn fifty, this is the test. Most insurances pay for all of it—mine did not. I really wanted to reschedule, but thankfully, the doctor understood my situation—three MRIs, one mammogram, two needle injections to the knee, physical therapy on my back this year alone, not to mention one sleep apnea test, one ultrasound of the heart, and one stress test for the husband. Hattiesburg is blessed to have such a wonderful medical community, and the clinic helped me with my payment.

Now this is where all the lemon lime comes into play. The day before the procedure is the clear liquid diet—lime Jell-O, lemon Jell-O, yellow Life Savers, green Life Savers, Sprite, etc. Yuck. If it had not been for the clear broth from Kobe's, a local hibachi grill, I would have starved. Just when I didn't think it could get any worse, the colonoscopy prep is—wait for it—lemon lime, a gallon of it. Somewhere around eleven o'clock that night, I began to hate life and all things lemon lime. I had turned into the toddler lying on the floor pitching a fit, refusing to drink any more lemon lime. This whole situation could have been prevented if only that stuff had tasted like Dr. Pepper or Barq's Root Beer.

The next morning, I was ready and headed to the clinic. It wasn't as bad as I thought it would be. In fact, if I had only liked lemon lime, this would have been a breeze. Soon, I had my paperwork completed, a beautiful hospital gown on, and my IV started—just waiting for my turn. Somewhere around the time when I had to ask my husband to stop using the stretcher railing as a drum set, I began to get nervous. "Are you sure this thing is not gonna hurt?" I asked him again. He just grinned. It was the sort of grin that said, "Remember when you laughed at me during my stress test?"

Let me just state for the record: when I change my mind, there is no changing it back. My husband knows this. I must have had that "I'm going home" look because he grabbed my hand and said the sweetest prayer. I remember telling him that if he has lied, I will settle on this matter when I get back home. A few minutes later, they came and wheeled me down the hall. I was talking to all the nurses and the doctor. We were having a real good conversation, and then guess what happened? I woke up back in my room. I remember nothing. Praise the Lord.

Seriously, folks, this test was a breeze. As I said earlier, if I had only liked lemon-lime flavor, it would have been nothing to it. If you are fifty and have not done this test yet, do so. It can save your life. The main man had a polyp removed during his first one when he turned fifty. I can't imagine what would have happened had he not had the procedure and that thing had turned to cancer. To the folks at Hattiesburg Clinic, I say thank you. Your staff was top-notch—from the front desk to the time they put me in the car. I cannot say enough good things about my doctor. I will forever be grateful to him. See you in ten years, doc, and see if you can get that prep in a root beer flavor by then.

If anyone needs us, Chris and I will try to enjoy the remainder of the year without needing anymore medical staff, but it is good to know they are there in case we do. Here's to 2015—the year we got old.

26

Remember the Baby

I have been struggling with my Christmas story this year. I even asked my family to help me remember some things from the past that I could share with you—nothing came to mind. I guess I may have already written down everything noteworthy. This morning, as I was standing in the kitchen making Christmas Eve dinner—yes, we are having our celebration tonight—I thought about how this holiday has changed for my family. Christmas has long since been about the presents under the tree or watching the kids running into the living room with big smiles and bright eyes. Such sweet thoughts are running through my mind right now.

Those kinds of memories have now been replaced with grown-up things—the dreaded card with money in it. After all, they are twenty-seven and twenty-six—it is time. Of course, the daughter frowned at the idea at first. "Mom, really?"

I will admit it was less stressful, until yesterday, when I found myself in the middle of the mall, shopping. "I can't do it, Chris. I just can't!" I had changed my mind; they were going to get a present, even if it was just one. I am not ready yet for that to stop. The thought of them not tearing open the wrapping paper—I could not do it.

Oh, past traditions, where have you gone? The yearly picture with Santa Claus, the handwritten letters to the North Pole, the cookies left by the tree, the opening of one gift on Christmas Eve, and the children hugging their new toys with excitement as they unwrapped the packages one by one have all been replaced. They have grown-up jobs and coworkers and work parties. Not to mention, there is now a girlfriend and a boyfriend who have entered our new holiday traditions. The little blond-headed boy and the big blue-eyed baby girl are now making memories of their own. It's a joyful thing to watch.

My husband and I shared a big laugh the other day as he recalled a memory from his past. "Come here, Chris, and sing 'Silent Night' for the family." His mother would say every year. Someone would place him high on a table, and the family would all gather around. A precious, precious tradition they enjoyed until little Chris's voice changed. I can just see my ADHD husband fidgeting on top of that table.

Yes, traditions change as the family changes. As the children turned to teenagers, we would load the car up with ski clothes, hats, and goggles and head out West for the holiday. On one particular Christmas, we met Klaus. He was in charge of the place we were going to park our camper for the duration of our vacation—picture National Lampoon's Vacation here. Yes, we could have written those movies ourselves. Christmas vacations were our new traditions, and we loved them. Klaus assured us via phone that our big diesel, four-door truck would have no trouble making it up the mountainside to his campground. Turns out our new friend lied as we found ourselves stuck, on a gravel road, inching our way toward a near-death adventure. At least I think it may have been gravel underneath the layers of ice and snow. You have not experienced Christmas until you are stuck on a mountainside, pulling a thirty-foot camper and inching your way back down to the bottom. Once it became obvious to everyone involved—Klaus, my husband, me, the kids, and all ten cars waiting to go up the mountainside behind us—Klaus decided it was our fault. In an effort to prevent our host from having to learn a real Mississippi redneck lesson that my husband was fixing to teach him, I hopped out of the truck. I needed to guide this baby back down and back down in a hurry. Since the main man was busy trying to keep the camper from plummeting off the side of the mountain, I knew I was going to have to help. Plan would have worked too if I hadn't accidentally buried myself in the snow. Turns out the pig trail was narrower than presumed. Like a yard dart being tossed from the heavens, my big old body disappeared into a snow-filled gully. "Save the children, Chris. Come back in the springtime and get my body." Oh, the memories.

Today, the kids will be here for supper. We will hand them the dreaded grown-up Christmas card with money. They will tear open the wrapping paper one more time for me, and I will once again video it. We will play a game of high chaparral, our new family tradition. We will laugh and share stories from the past.

Christmas memories and traditions will change. I will try not to fret over it. One thing is for sure, and that is the reason for the season will forever be about the baby. Let's not forget that. It's the one traditional that we should never change. Thank you for following along with my crazy life. We wish you and your family a very Merry Christmas (2015).

27

New York City, Here I Come!

New York City Bestseller Secrets and Book Signing—it will be fun, they said. Wanna go? Well, shoot yeah, I do. It was a slam-packed weekend—a movie producer, media consultant, radio talk-show host, literary agent, and CEOs from a top publishing company. What more could a small-town writer ask for, right? So I begin to save my money and pay for this sure-to-be a grand adventure. If you have been following me for any amount of time, then you know my adventures are always how short stories are made. This one would be no exception.

Everyone on my Facebook page began to count the days down. A country-gone-to-town moment was about to happen, and they did not want to miss one minute of it. I prayed God would send the money. My friends prayed too. A few days before my big departure, it became obvious a snowstorm was brewing. Have no fear! I survived Hurricane Katrina, so what's a little snow. Besides, it will be beautiful to see—cold, but beautiful nonetheless.

This once-in-a-lifetime moment became even better when my daughter was able to go with me. The trip down to New Orleans airport was windy—very windy—but other than that, uneventful, and I was not nervous about flying. Of course, there was the slight embarrassment to the daughter when the TSA folks randomly picked me for a pat down. "Stop acting so nervous, Mom. They are going to pick you every time." She fretted. But I can't help it. I'm going to NYC.

The captain of the JetBlue Airlines held steady in the windy skies. The flight attendant—is that the correct title now—offered drinks and snacks. I accepted. After all, I am going to make the most of this adventure, for I'm not sure there will ever be another one. As the plane began preparing for landing, I will admit the heartbeat raced a little, but the captain nailed it without any problems.

As we departed into the big city, our first order of business was the taxi. For those of you, like me, who are not that familiar with airports and taxis, let me explain. Once you retrieve your luggage from the carousel, you walk outside and hail a cab. Ta-da! It's that easy. Apparently, this is where I embarrassed the daughter for the second time. "How long will it take to get to the hotel?" I asked. I still find no problem with this question, for we needed to remain on schedule. I do not want to miss one minute of this learning experience. Imagine my surprise when the driver answered, "One hour." Wait, what? Sweet heavens above. Just what state did our plane land in? One hour? Why on earth did we land so far away? Turns out we didn't—only seventeen miles but the traffic was bumper to bumper. It's all part of big city living. Another thing to note about the traffic, close your eyes. Don't look. It's what nightmares are made of.

Since the Friday night conference was a dinner meeting held at the Pier A Harbor House, first, let me tell you about the menu. The appetizer: baby arugula and endive salad with local goat cheese, walnut, and Chardonnay vinaigrette. Followed by the entrée: green circle chicken breast, spinach, garlic potato puree, and rosemary jus. Lastly, dessert: warm chocolate cake, Baci ice cream, butterscotch sauce. I am going to keep it real, folks, and confess I have no idea what some of that stuff was, but I found myself wanting to lick the plate when I was finished. I didn't, though. Although raised in the trailer park, I do have manners.

The biggest snowstorm since the eighteen-hundreds was fast approaching. I will say Tate Publishing was diligent in keeping our group up-to-date. The guest speakers were adjusted between the scheduled meetings in order for them to return home safely. It was certainly understandable and no one had a problem with rearranging the speakers for sure. We were all excited to be there.

Kevin McAfee, CEO and Founder of Veritas Entertainment, was up first. Following Kevin was none other than Molly Polcari. She is the person you need to know if you want to be successful promoting your books on the television. I was glued to every word they said. Why, you ask? Because I plan on having my book made into a movie one day, that's why. I need Kevin and Molly. By the time those two finished, I felt like I had brought a connect-the-dot coloring book to a Picasso exhibit. "What's your passion about?" they asked. Clearly, I was at the wrong conference. Molly said to know your material. Be an expert. Keep learning. When the time came, you don't want to miss the opportunity to speak on the subject. Whoa! I have no subject. I have failed them tremendously, only Ryan Tate does not realize it yet. My best bet is to sit back and be quiet. Maybe they won't notice me and all my crayons.

Later that evening was my first New York City book signing. I, Vicki Baylis, from the trailer park, was in New York City, signing books—books I have written. I have tears trying to escape thinking about that. Crowded does not begin to describe that coffee shop. I loved every minute of it, but I could not help but continue to think about my passion. I honestly did not know or did I have time to fret over it either. As soon as the book signing was over, we headed to the top of the Empire State Building. If you get the chance to do that, do so. Go at night, in the snow. You will never forget it.

I fell asleep worrying over my passion or my lack of one. How can I be an author—an expert—on anything, when I don't know what my passion is? Molly will never call upon me to speak. I have nothing important to say, unlike the others who have written about wars and political stuff and major news events that are happening now.

Bright and early the next morning, we hurried downstairs. I may not be like the other authors, but I still have a desire to learn all I can about writing. Believe it or not, it was in the lobby that I discovered my passion. You all know how I love to talk, and I found myself talking to Stu Taylor. Yes, you heard me correctly—Stu Taylor, the nationally syndicated talk-show host. I told him I was worried I did not have a newsworthy passion like the others. I will never be on the curvy couch of Fox News discussing world events or the latest political topics. My passion is my family, and that is what my books are about: family. Mistakes that are made, milestones that are achieved, goals that are dreamed, days that are lived, laughs that are shared, problems that are solved, and hugs that are given. You want to know what Stu said when I told him my passion was my family? "That's the best kind of passion there is," he said. "The best kind of passion there is." So if Molly ever needs someone to talk about struggling with household bills and other everyday problems that we all face, I'm the gal for the job. Until then, I will just keep writing.

I put the smile back on my face, and we all headed to breakfast. Like the first meeting, this one too was centered around the dining room table, kind of like we do here in the South. Dr. Tate joined us. I don't know how, but he made us all feel like family; we talked, and laughed, and listened to the speakers. Just when it could not get any better, Dr. Tate approached the podium himself. Have you ever been in church and God seems to be talking through the preacher directly at you? Like someone has tattled and you are looking around the church trying to figure out who told on you? His message was as passionate as I have ever seen spoken. You want to know what he talked about? His family and the struggles he faced being a new author. I kid you not. It was tailor-made for me. He too had a desire to write books, and he also had bills, and hardships, and kids to deal with. He too didn't know if the books would sell or if the utilities would get paid. He was just like me, and look where he is now. I'm really not talking about the success of his books or his company either. I'm talking about the success of his family.

I cannot say the rest of the day was uneventful. After all, we were in the midst of a major blizzard. Although our dinner cruise was cancelled by the coast guard and I did not get to sit on the curvy couch at Fox News, we still had a blast. We toured the NBC studio. I did let the tour guides know they will be seeing me again when I become rich and famous. They would let Jimmy know to be expecting me.

My hats off to Brittany Fisher, Mark Mingle, and Kole Melton. They faced every obstacle the storm threw at them with such grace and dignity. I want Ryan Tate to know he has the best of the best working with him—never saw weakness, only the love of Jesus Christ working through them. I'm sure we, the authors—and I am mainly talking about myself—were like herding chickens all weekend long. I know they probably continued to hear me in their sleep. "Y'all don't lose me in this city." If I said it once, I said it a hundred times. I feared I would be riding the subway all night if they didn't watch me close enough.

Remember when I said I had been through Hurricane Katrina so a little snow would not be a big deal? I lied. One by one, the transportation systems were being shut down. The last few hundred feet to the hotel was on foot. Folks, it was as if we were inside a snow globe and someone was shaking the stew out of it. Lord, have mercy, we could not see two inches in front of us. Somewhere between the two feet of snow on the ground and the stinging snow flurries piercing my face, Rebekah and I veered off course. "Mom!" my daughter yelled. "I'm in the water." She wasn't the only one. How on earth did we stumble into the Hudson River, I wondered. "Swim, child, swim!" Best I can tell is we walked right into a water fountain of some sort. I will say it gave a whole new meaning to the word *ice cold*. I have never departed from soggy clothes as fast as I did that night.

The word *successful* is not based on what others think it is for you. It is what *you* decide it to be. I will continue to write books about my family, and I will share them with you too. When I have left this earthly world, my books will still be here. You will have no doubt in your mind what my passion was—my family. Thank you, Tate Publishing, for such a wonderful weekend. Thank you for letting me be one of your authors. My name is Vicki Baylis. I am an author, and my family is my passion.

28

Ridin' in Style

I think everyone knows that God answers prayers. Sometimes, the answer is yes, and sometimes, the answer is no. I've had several of those answers that were no. I am not going to pretend those don't hurt either because they do. Honestly, sometimes, a *no* can be the best thing to ever happen in your life—you can thank God that I am not a country music star. Even though I thought the Man upstairs was crazy for that not happening, I can't sing. I know that now. He knew it back then.

I recall once Chris and I found this piece of property for sale and we just had to have it. It was perfect. So like any young couple, we took a grown-up out to confirm our expert opinion. In our case, it was our banker, Mr. Fairley. After all, it would be him who would be lending us the money for this sure-to-be wise investment. As we walked around the property, showing him all the good things, he listened. You know what happened? God said no and He used our banker to tell us that. What? A short time later, we realized how foolish we were for thinking that home was our mansion on earth. In fact, it was only a step or two above run-down looking. We would probably still be living there all these years later because there was no way on earth we could have found another idiot couple to buy it from us. Whew! We dodged a bullet there.

There are many examples of how God knows what is best. For as long as I can remember, I have dreamed of buying an RV. I want to travel around this great country riding in style. Oh, the writing I could do in one of those things. So far, the funds for this dream are just not there. In fact, those funds—well, let's just say that God has a sense of humor sometimes. For the last decade, my prayers have been focused on funding stuff like the power bill, the kids' college tuition, car maintenance, my doctor bills, and the grocery list—which we sometimes refer to as the wish list behind the magnet on the refrigerator door. Now don't get me wrong, our needs have been met. They may be embarrassingly past due, but they are being met, no doubt.

Sometimes, your wishes are met in the most surprising ways, which is the case with my RV. God provided me with one—a free one. Seriously, free. Let me explain. It is the most beautiful thing on wheels—FR3 by Forest River. It is thirty feet long and has everything I have ever dreamed of. Only it belongs to my cousin Cindy and that man she married. They were recently blessed with buying one. And the best part, I get to travel everywhere they go for free. Of course, we split the gas bill and the groceries and the park fees, but other than that, it is free. God is good. I never dreamed it would happen this way—His way—the best way.

Before I tell you about the maiden voyage down the highway in this mansion on wheels, let me back this story up a few decades. Cindy and I may not be perfect, but there is one thing you will have to admit about us—we put our kids first. Yes, ma'am. Our world revolved around our husbands and our kids. This week, Cindy's son moved into his new house—weeks shy of the arrival of his firstborn child. Last weekend, a baby shower was given, and let me tell you that young couple was blessed with tons and tons of new baby stuff. I'll admit some of these newfangled contraptions I do not understand. How on earth did I get my babies raised without all that stuff is beyond me. I was honored to help tote all those shower gifts into the new baby's room. I am so thankful God has blessed that young family.

Which gets me to the reason I brought this up. I remember hauling my young'uns all over the place. At first, it was car seats, diaper bags, and bottles. Then it was life jackets, grills, and the boat. As they grew, it became ski equipment, snow bibs, goggles, and trips out west to the ski lodges. Everything focused on them and what their dad and I could show them. We have been to tops of mountains, underground lakes, viewing the ocean floor with glass-bottom boats, fishing expeditions, hiking trails, bear watching, etc. It would take weeks and sometimes months of planning, budgeting, packing, and cooking casseroles to put in the freezer to feed our families while we hauled the campers across this land. Cindy and I would not change any of that for the world, but now that the kids are grown, it is our turn.

One evening, a few days after they bought this magnificent dream on wheels, we said, "Let's go camping in the new RV." Here's the funny part—deciding where. She was at her house packing, and I was at mine packing too—clothes, blood pressure pills, back pain and sinus meds, reading glasses, hearing aid batteries, bacon, eggs, milk, bread, cookies, hard candy, chips, nabs, chocolate, and a list of old folk's items that goes on and on. If you are my age, you know what I'm talking about. Then someone said, "How about the Alamo?" So it was—we headed to Texas.

It did not take me long to realize why God had said no to my getting an RV for all these years. Let me paint the picture. The captain chairs are where my husband and that man my cousin married sat during this adventure. Cindy and I chose the couch—it had reclining leg rests on them. It was heaven on earth. It was the perfect seats if you want to view the world from the comfort of reclining chairs. Then it happened. "You know the kitchen table has seat belts too? Let's try them out." So we did. You want to know what sitting at the kitchen table feels like as you are traveling down the highway? It's like sitting inside the snack pantry of your house. Since the cabinets were within arm's reach, we snacked all the way through Texas. Lord, have mercy. If God had answered my prayers for a motor home years ago, I'd be ordering my clothes from a tentmaker right about now.

Let me tell you some of the highlights of ridin' in style. For starters, if you are on a fluid pill for slightly high blood pressure, you don't have to stop the vehicle at a restroom every twenty miles. If you get hungry, just stretch your arm out, the cabinet is right there. If you are thirsty, there's a fridge full of cold drinks to your right. You want to take a nap, grab a pillow off the bed. If you want to set up camp, press a button from your captain chair; this thing levels its own self. If you want to make the room bigger, there is a button for that too. You need to back that baby up—there is a camera back there that helps you. RVs are just as I imagined them to be—perfect. And this one was even better than perfect—it was free to me.

As we rolled that big boy into San Antonio, Texas, we soon realized something we had not thought of: football—a championship game to be exact. It turned out football is well loved in the state of Texas. Since Cindy and I had snacked all the way from Mississippi, we were ready for something hearty to eat, like a steak. As we strolled down the River Walk—it's a popular place to shop, eat, and walk—you know what we found? We found everybody. Yes, everybody. All of Texas. And they all wanted a steak too, like a bunch of ants on a hot sidewalk except it wasn't hot. Instead, it was cold and raining. Goodness, you could not have squeezed another soul into that city. One hour and forty-five minutes after we added our name to the waiting list, we were told it would be another thirty minutes. Thirty more minutes? Oh, heck, no. I don't know how y'all do it out here, but back in Mississippi, I would have had my supper dishes already cleaned and put up four hours ago. "Just how much against the law is it to start pushing these folks into the little river?" Since I wanted to sleep in the RV and not the county jail, we cancelled our steak reservation and headed back to the RV for leftovers. One day, I want to go back and have one of those fancy steaks, preferable when all of Texas is not there.

It was an honor to visit the Alamo. I count it as one of my most cherished places I have visited. The folks in San Antonio were top-notch if you can overlook their love for football and steaks. If you get to visit, make sure you stop by Lulu's for the cinnamon roll. I recommend fasting forty days prior to ordering it. You will thank me later. As we slowly made our way back to the Magnolia state, we stopped in Temple, Texas. Actually, the GPS had us wandering aimlessly through the Lone Star State for hours, and we just ended up there. I think it was because God wanted us to enjoy all the deer. The campground was full of them, just walking around, enjoying life.

You want to know how hard that was for a Mississippi redneck not to wish he had his rifle with him? Ask my husband.

I guess the reason for this story is to let you know that God does in fact answer our prayers. Sometimes, it is yes; sometimes, it is no. And sometimes, it is even better than we ask for. Even at age fifty-one, I still find myself learning new things. These past couple of months have been hard. I found out it is much easier to have God say no to me than it is to watch God say no to my children. It was much harder. Words can't describe the feeling. But I do know this, and I want my kids to know this: He is in control, and He knows what we do not yet understand. Like with the dilapidated house we almost mortgaged up to our eyeballs, I am thankful for His *no*. Today, we may not understand, but one day, we will. If you happen to see an FR3 Forest River RV with a Forrest County tag headed down the highway, honk your horn. It may be me and Cindy. You will be witnessing with your own eyes one of God's answers to me—it was a no, but it is so much better than a yes.

29

Thought I Was a Caroline

If there is one thing I hate, it is admitting I was wrong. There! I said it. I, Vicki Baylis, was wrong. Now don't misunderstand me, I am not lazy. Well, at least not up until I injured my knee in the parking lot incident months ago. Ever since then, I have been walking around as if I am a few days away from life in the nursing home. That being said, I am not by nature a lazy human being. I know how to cook, clean, garden, and mow the yard. I sort of considered myself a Caroline Ingalls type of gal, so to speak. For all you young whipper-snappers, Caroline Ingalls was the Ma from the *Little House on the Prairie* series years ago. You know back when we watched the television because of good acting talent and not because of all the shock value stuff we see today. Nothing chaps me more than watching a good ole Western today and have to listen to all the F-bombs being dropped left and right by not only the men but the women too. Just ruins it all. I just can't believe that word was so popular back in the day. It's kind of like watching Caroline Ingalls pop her chicken into a microwave to cook. Keep it real, folks. Okay, enough about that soapbox. Moving on to the next one.

Let me back this story up a bit. I am in the middle of reading Ramona Bridges' book titled *Sweet By and By*. Lord, have mercy, I cannot put it down. It was based in the good ole days when women really had to work at keeping their children dressed and fed. You know, sewing britches, making quilts, canning peaches, and wring-ing the chicken's neck? Unlike it is today, back then, it was hard being a woman. As hard as it was, they still made it to church on Sunday. Mostly, I think it was to ask the Good Lord to help keep them from killing other folks. Take for instant this week at my house. I have failed at my household duties—thanks in part to Ramona and her book. While her characters were busy as bees tending to their houses, I had my feet propped up reading about it. I even sent my husband and my son to the grocery store for me. Do not judge—you haven't read Ramona's book yet. It's that good. When my son called me from the deli to confirm I wanted to pay forty dollars for the whole block of cheddar cheese and another forty for a block of American cheese, sliced, I put the book down. I did not want by any means eighty dollars' worth of cheese. I immediately retook the grocery shopping back from them.

While my family was not starving by any means, they had been getting the bare minimum, unlike the women in Ramona's book. Even though they were in the middle of canning season, and hog killings, and squirrel hunting, and boiling water outside for washing clothes, those women could still put a meal on the table. Talk about ruining a good lazy spell—that book did it. I commenced to planning a meal fitting of a real housewife—a Caroline Ingalls kind of housewife. Right down to the homemade peach cobbler. Yes, sir. I am woman. Only I almost set the kitchen on fire again in the process with all my skillet frying. I have never understood why I cannot fry food. Fried pork chops—nope. Fried chicken—nope. Fried cube steak—nope. Fried okra—nope. Well, to be honest, if I was only frying the okra, I can do that, but if I have to add anything else to the equation, then I'm breaking out the fire extinguisher and hoping the fire department can make it on time if necessary. I looked like one of those hibachi chefs with spoons and knives slinging everywhere, getting more nervous with each passing minute. Just like my past attempts, my kitchen started smoking and looking like the inside of a bar—you know, back before they started making everyone smoke their cigarettes outside. Once again, my husband walked in, started raising windows, and announced, "It's a little cloudy in here, isn't it." I didn't have time to talk or to even give him the evil eye. Apparently,

I mismeasured and was too busy making enough gravy to feed the entire neighborhood.

I sat down at the dinner table still wearing my yellow apron with my hair looking like I had been strapped to the outside of a rocket. I'll admit, I love aprons, but honestly, I may need to invest in some sort of OSHA outfit if I want to keep attempting to fry foods. I'm not even going to bring up the fact that I didn't have to go down to the barn and chase a chicken down or, worse, kill a hog.

It did bring lots of laughter and good memories to the table while we ate supper, though. Once when the kids were teenagers, I set the stove on fire. When the kitchen finally cleared that night, my husband tried to use it as a learning experience for the children. "What do you do if the grease catches on fire?" he asked them. This is where I know I cloned my daughter because she blurted out, "Throw vegetable oil on it!" which, for the record, is not the answer.

After all these years of thinking I was Caroline Ingalls, I admit I was wrong. For all you chicken-feather-plucking, squirrel-huntin', hog-killing women out there in this world, I salute you. If you need me, I'll be over at Oleson Mercantile having coffee with Harriet and discussing Ramona's new book.

30

Sitting at the Kitchen Table

Last night, Brother Bill and his family joined us for supper—his birthday meal—table for eight right in the middle of my kitchen. As always, the entire evening was filled with lots of laughter. If there is one thing my family is blessed to the max with, it is laughter. Of course, supper wasn't anything fancy—sloppy joes, cowboy beans, and hash brown casserole all being served on paper plates. Somewhere during our fancy dining experience, the topic of killing hogs came up. Bill said not too long ago our mother mentioned a hog-killing event from her past. "From the rooter to the tooter," my husband recalled his grandpa saying about hog-killing.

This conversation led us to remember some things about sitting around our mother's supper table. Now don't get me wrong, Mother knew how to make a meal out of flour and water, and there were many times she did just that too. There were other times when she reached back into the good ole days and put it right on our kitchen table—beef liver, chicken livers, and fried oysters. I'm gonna be the first to admit, when I raised my kids, we had a rule at my table: you must at least eat a bite of it no matter what. Now before all you "I just want to be friends with my kids" kind of parents go reporting me to social services about mistreating my own flesh and blood, know that it didn't cause them any lasting harm. I was their mother, not their childhood friend. Besides, that's the only way you will ever know if you like something or not. I'll get back to this philosophy shortly.

The rule when we were kids was you sat there and finished your plate before you got up—there, that's what therapy sessions should be filled with. Momma didn't play that friend game with her young'uns. No, sir, she was the mother, and we were the kids, and we was gonna learn to love liver and onions. Oh, the wasted yard-playing time spent sitting at her table, looking at our plates—always just me and Bill. Terri seemed to have no problem cleaning her plate, but then again, the princess was the only one allowed to get up from the table and "check" on Tinkerbell, the family cat. We have our suspicions. "Mommy, can I check on Tinkerbell?" My precious little sister would ask. Last night, it all came back—Tinkerbell was fat as a tick on liver and onion day, fat as a tick. That sassy-britches little sister of ours had outsmarted us both.

Rebekah and her boyfriend, Nathan, spent the last two summers traveling to South America. I'm not going to say exactly which countries because I do not wish to offend anyone or their customs. While my daughter was scrubbing the germs off her apple, so to speak, Nathan was chowing down on sushi being sold on sidewalks. Even the locals were saying, "No, señor, don't do it." I bet Nathan's mom had the same rule at her house—try everything once—and Nathan did from alpacas to lizards. In the open meat markets, you know how to tell if the meat is fresh? If the flies are still sitting on it. Let that sink in, will you?

According to my brother, the only thing worse than beef liver is cold beef liver after you stare at it for at least thirty minutes. Then he remembered a trip down to our aunt's house where he was introduced to tripe. You may give it a fancy name, but in the end, it is still a cow's stomach. I don't know how y'all were raised, but we grew up where the house rules extended outside the house. Yes, sir, you behave everywhere you went, and that included your aunt's house too. Bill said he didn't want to spend thirty minutes sitting at her table, so he set out to get it done—just wolf it down. It was like chewing on a bicycle inner tube—could not be done. "I'm gonna tell you, there is no fast way to eat tripe," he said. We all laughed and laughed as he retold the story.

Then my son, Eli, spoke. He had a similar experience with a goat esophagus. Yep, a goat esophagus. In one village, it was a delicacy—a dessert. After two goats were killed to feed the entire village, a man walked around with it, cutting little pieces off as he went. As you may recall, my son has lived all over the world, and he loved every moment of it. In one village, the guest of honor was in charge of killing the chicken before the meal. So he did. It is humbling to know in villages where poverty is raging among the people they welcome their guest with open arms, sharing all they have to offer. We, as Americans, could stand to know about this kind of love. They spoiled him rotten—treating him like a king—according to their standards. The guest of honor is given the best they have to offer: the organ meat—eyeballs, brains, gizzards, livers. "I never ate a solid piece of chicken meat the whole time I was there. I was too busy eating the organs of honor." It's a good thing I taught my kids to try everything once. He would have starved over there otherwise.

I guess the reason for this story is to say we really should not complain about what is sitting on our own kitchen tables. Instead, we should give thanks because it could be worse—much worse. I admit I am one of the worst about this. Back when the economy was awful for us, the main man and I ate enough mac and cheese to feed an army. I have not bought a box of that stuff since.

There are so many around us with empty tables. Just like in the villages my children traveled in, we should share our blessing with others. It may not always be steak and lobster, but I guarantee you it will be enough to share with others. Just a thought.

I want to wish my little brother a very happy fiftieth birthday. Welcome to old age. It's all downhill from here on out. Love you lots, Brother Bill.

31

The Airstream

I don't know where to start this story. I guess let me begin with the fact we are selling our house. It's been on the market for a while, but it will sell eventually. I have faith. The main man and I want to live on a few acres in the country. I dream daily of having chickens, a few goats, cows, and a little garden. In the meantime, I will continue to enjoy the beautiful porches of my two-story three-bedroom, two-bath house with hardwood flooring that overlooks the lake. See what I did there? Call me to schedule your private viewing.

Anyway, back to the story. Where to start, where to start? My son wanted an Airstream camper. Apparently, remodeling one of them is the new cool thing to do. Besides, he is going to live in it when it's completed. It is cheaper than paying rent, and wherever his next job takes him, his new home will go too. Like with everything he does, he researched and researched and researched. He soon found one in Florida. "Hey, Dad, can you and Uncle BC go with me to make sure it's the right one?" Turns out he thought it was perfect, and we hauled that silver baby back here to Mississippi. Of course, my brother said it looked more in need of a resurrecting than a remodeling. Within two days, the child of mine had taken it completely apart and scattered it all over the yard—looked like it had exploded into five thousand pieces. Oh yeah, the house is sure to sell now. I have faith he will be able to put it all back together eventually. A few months back, he successfully took apart his four-wheeler, two motorcycles, and one

El Camino in order to refurbish and sell them. My garage has been turned into a mechanic's dream. *This house will never sell.*

I'll have you know we whipped out the checkbook; the endless purchasing began—new flooring, new appliances, new paint, new heating and air, etc. Next, we hired the best of the best in contractors—painters, welders, electricians, and plumbers. Within thirty minutes, this project was complete, and my son pulled the beautiful Airstream camper out of our driveway and began his own journey. Yeah, right. Let me remind you we are the Baylises—the broke Baylises—and it didn't happen anywhere near that scenario. When you are broke, you have to be creative. It takes elbow grease and a whole lot of prayer. I like to think it was a learning experience for everyone involved, whether we wanted the learning or not, we got it.

First on the list was the welding. In all honesty, I don't know how we didn't drop pieces of the frame all along the interstate while getting it to my yard. All I can figure is God was holding his hands underneath the rusted metal frame as we traveled. If we had only known what the trailer frame looked like before we pulled out of Florida, we would have walked that baby back to Mississippi—carrying garbage bags—waiting for the pieces to drop off. I will say Eli did an excellent job learning how to weld. It took a little while, but he got it done.

After weeks of saving his money, he found the flooring. Since his house is not very big, he was able to get really nice floors on sale from the clearance section. It's a miracle. God is good. Oh, how those floors shined. You know what happened next? Cue the rain. There was massive rain—like Noah-build-another-Ark kind of rain. Every time Eli thought he had the roof leaks fixed, another one would appear— the poor beautiful wood floor. I'm stressing—Eli was not. One day, I waded out to the "jobsite" and looked inside. It saddened my heart a little to see my son sitting on the floor, back leaned against the bare wall, legs stretched out in front, looking a little overwhelmed. It was sad. The floor needed to come up—well, a big section of it did. The rainwater had trickled down the wall and seeped under the hardwood flooring. No matter how old your children get, when they are faced with a broken heart, you hurt too. As a mother, you must hide your tears, give them a hug, and encourage them forward. "You can handle this, son. It's just a little bump in the road."

There were many more bumps to come, though; he was laid off from his job. The little money he had to remodel his new home became even less. I admit I secretly cried a few tears over the news. Let me evoke a mother's bragging right here—my son is very talented. You would not believe the comments I hear from other professionals in his field when someone realizes I am his mother. You will never hear Eli bragging on himself, though. Years ago, I dropped by his place of work to look inside the media world. "You want these things, Mom?" he said. It was a stack of photojournalism awards he had received over the years. He never mentioned getting them. He was so talented and yet so laid off. Once again, I said, "It's just a little bump in the road." It's hard to see God's plan sometimes.

For a few weeks, everyone focused on the Airstream and not worrying so much about finding another job. He had faith God would send a good one. I did too. Piece by piece, the silver bullet was returning to its glory. The wiring, the walls, the ceiling were done. Next on the list was finding cabinets. This is where we knew God must have been watching the Airstream get remodeled too. Lowe's—oh, how we love Lowe's. Sitting right smack dab on the clearance aisle was a kitchen cabinet, slightly damaged, but to my son, it was perfect. One cabinet installed. If we could only find another one just like it, and we did a couple of weeks later. Where? On the damaged aisle of another Lowe's store. God is good.

Have you ever heard the saying, "You can tell what's inside someone's heart by how they handle getting their thumb smashed with a hammer?" On the day we were painting the cabinets, I saw Eli's heart. "Mom, can you hand me that towel?" he said calmly, as I turned around to see a full can of white paint spread all over his beautiful hardwood floors. The bumps seemed endless to me, but he never complained, never gave up. In my opinion, this kind of heart comes from knowing what true hardships are. While traveling all over the world, he saw them firsthand—real poverty, real sickness, real hunger, real hurt, and real sorrow. It makes roof leaks and spilled paint seem unimportant.

Each step of the way, we became better and better at remodeling on a dime—clearance aisles, scrap pieces of this and that given to us for free, and junkyards. It's the junkyard I want to tell you about. We found one nearby, and according to the guy on the phone, there were several RVs in there too. First, let me say that when you are visiting a scrapyard, wear the appropriate shoes—take it from me when I say open-toed sandals are not recommended. Secondly, I can tell you it was not a woman that designed junkyards, for if it had been, it would have looked a whole lot different. A woman would have placed the broken down cars in some sort of order—size, color, type, make, and model. There would have been sidewalks, paved roads, and street signs to prevent you from wandering aimlessly around the miles and miles of endless broken down, crinkled up, and rusted out piles of metal. There would have been golf carts. Restrooms and refreshment stands would be scattered among the acres and acres of the scary untamed wilderness.

Speaking of scary, if you have teenagers on the verge of getting their driver's license, take them on a tour of a junkyard. Let them see firsthand that tragic car wrecks knows no boundaries—rich cars, big cars, old cars, tiny cars, all seem to have the same ability to end up a wrecked mangled mess of metal. There are no social boundaries here. As we continued to walk through, I began to sense the sadness of each vehicle and the toll it must have taken on all the humans involved. The quiet eeriness was as thick as fog on a Mississippi pond. If I had seen this years ago, I would have never agreed to let my kids have a driver's license.

Anyway, back to my story. We found several beat-up and burned out RVs. I ventured into the first one we stumbled upon. After that, my husband was on his own. Been there once and that was enough—spiders, snakes, bugs, not to mention rusted metal—it was a tetanus shot just waiting to happen, and I wanted no part of it. The only thing that could make this long and tiresome dusty road walk any worse was rain, which is exactly what happened next. Take me home, Jesus. It is safe to say I am not a junkyard-pickin' kind of woman. Felt like I was lost in a desert dragging my empty canteen behind me as I stumbled around yelling, "Water, water, water." There had to be an easier way of getting this Airstream back together.

As me and my wet, dirty feet were standing there in the middle of the road pleading to go home, he insisted on one more. Through the briars and overgrown weeds, he cautiously made his way inside the lopsided RV. "Don't do it!" I insisted, to no avail. I'll confess it now. When I heard him yell for help followed by a loud crashing sound that I could only assume was the bottom of the camper giving way, I hesitated. Actually, it was more like I ignored it. He was on his own. I told him not to go in there in the first place. I would have called 911, but let's face it, I didn't know where we were; we had been lost for two hours. Besides, they would have never found us before nightfall, and I had no intentions of being in this graveyard in the dark. "Man up in there, Chris!" I did my best to encourage him. By the time he crawled out of the floor and back through the jungle, he was ready to go home too. It was almost enough to cause a Baptist to partake of the liquor. It is difficult being broke sometimes.

Now let me get to the part where God showed back up. Once the media world found out my son was looking for a job, his phone started ringing off the hook. It was amazing to see God's plan in action—offers pouring in left and right. We are so thankful for each one of those job offerings. After careful thought, he chose the one he felt was the best for him. The Airstream is almost finished—some plumbing left to do and the windows need curtains. Does it have everything on his wish list? Not yet, but to my son, it is perfect. In a few days, the silver bullet will leave my yard and travel up the highway. May God continue to watch over my son. It may be just an Airstream camper to everyone else, but to my son, it is home.

32

Things That Make You Go Hmmm

My son and the Airstream camper have arrived to their new destination. It is customary when my children move out of the house or move to another location far from us, we will buy them a buggy full of groceries. I won't have them going hungry while they are waiting on the first paycheck, you know? When my son graduated college and took a job in Vicksburg, we helped him move. Then we took him on a trip to Walmart. "Okay, fill the buggy up with whatever you want," my husband said. "Then we're going to cut the apron string," he continued with a laugh or two. I will say my daughter figured out how to stretch the apron string as far as possible. While she was in graduate school, her daddy continued to fill up her grocery buggy once a month.

Our plan was to leave early morning, but due to last-minute adjustments on the camper—gas water heater, plumbing, and electrical stuff, not to mention loading it up with everything my son owns—we didn't pull out until lunchtime. Turns out that was a good thing due to the strong storm making its way across our state. Anybody else tired of the rain? I know I am. Not sure what has happened but my yard lost a lot of grass—bare spots everywhere. No idea why. I would scream up and ask God to stop it—just stop it with all the rain before my beautiful grass disappears completely, but I don't want to be responsible for the Mississippi Drought of 2016 in case He gets mad at me for complaining.

Anyway, as the men were trampling mud onto the waxed camper floors, I was sitting on the front porch, praying. Lord, help us to have a safe trip. Keep a watch over the storms as we travel up the highway. Be with Eli as he is driving the camper. And God did. I watched the weather app on my phone on the way up Highway 49. It was truly amazing to see the radar green and red all around but never on top of us, like a bubble of clear skies surrounding the silver bullet all the way.

Once the camper was hooked up—water, electricity, and leveled—we set out for lunch at 4:30 p.m. Keeping with tradition, off to the grocery store we went. I'm not sure I can adequately describe what happened next, but let me start with the fact both my kids are from this new generation. In fact, my daughter is a vegetarian. Makes my head spin, but I certainly understand. She is plagued with migraines, and this kind of diet helps keep her headaches under control. The son, on the other hand, will eat everything in sight except for tuna and spaghetti. Tuna, he just does not care for, and while he lived out of our great country, he lived on spaghetti; therefore, he cannot eat another bite of it. Don't get me wrong, though, if he is invited at your table and spaghetti is served, you will never know he does not like it—yes, he was raised right.

Let me paint the scene. The buggies in this grocery store are tiny. Not like the big shopping carts you push around through the aisles of Walmart. No, sir, tiny. Into the fresh fruits and vegetable section we go. Nothing unusual here as my son checks out the produce. Next up, cheese. I will say the cheese area was a beautiful eye-catching display of every kind of cheese known to mankind—blocks, slices, and shredded; at least I think there may have been shredded. In all honesty, I went into some kind of sticker shock. Eight dollars for a few slices of cheese? Wait, what is happening? Where's the Kraft and the cellophane wrappers? "Eli, this must be the fancy cheese section for the rich folks. Let's see if we can find the regular cheese." I'll have you know we searched and searched that store over for the regular cheese section—you know for the common folks—it ain't there. Lord, have mercy on my pocketbook as my son began to toss the fancy cheese blocks and slices into our buggy. It was here that my husband and I realized we were in trouble. This was not like a regular store. Standing at the meat counter is where I asked God, "Why couldn't you have made this one the vegetarian?" Somewhere after we noticed the buffalo meat and the make-your-own peanut butter stand, the main man left this shopping adventure. He had noticed a few tables and chairs at the front of the store—he needed to sit down—leaving me to push the buggy through the land of disbelief. I had long since given up trying to estimate the cost and threw caution to the wind. If my debit card don't catch on fire when we check out of this place, I guess all will be okay.

Raise your hand if you have ever bought beans and oatmeal by the pound. Yes, sir, just place a bag under the dispenser and fill it up. When we finally navigated over to the soups, I breathed a sigh of relief—it was on sale, for three dollars each. I kid you not. Not to be outdone by the massive soup sale, the frozen burritos was a steal—six of them for just slightly under twenty-five dollars. Aren't we lucky? Has this place never heard of sunbeam, frosted flakes, hamburger helper, Borden's, or Campbell's? You may not be able to buy a bag of Chips Ahoy cookies here, but if you got the money, you can take home an octopus—legs and all. "You touch anything in this seafood section, young man, and I'll throw one of these high-dollar cans of soup at your head." Honestly, at this point, a trip to the emergency room with a concussion while I run and fill up a buggy at Walmart would still be cheaper than this store.

He was all smiles, grinning from ear to ear, while unloading his buggy full of healthy eating. I, on the other hand, was having a mini Pentecostal revival inside my body. "Work a miracle, Lord, work a miracle!" If He can part the Red Sea, He can surely make the cost of this buggy less than my monthly house note. Right before the last item was scanned, my son turned and said, "Mom, I know this is going to cost too much money. I'll pay for some of it." We may have a tuna fish budget, but both my children have hearts of gold. If I have to choose where I want my blessings to be—with my checking account or with my children—I will always choose my children.

CPSIA information can be obtained
at www.ICGtesting.com
Printed in the USA
FSHW02n1350100618
49080FS